4th Workshop on Innovative Use of NLP for Building Educational Applications 2009

Held at NAACL HLT 2009

Boulder, Colorado, USA
5 June 2009

ISBN: 978-1-61738-567-4

Printed from e-media with permission by:

Curran Associates, Inc.
57 Morehouse Lane
Red Hook, NY 12571

Some format issues inherent in the e-media version may also appear in this print version.

Printed by Curran Associates, Inc. (2010)

Association for Computational Linguistics
209 N. Eighth Street
Stroudsburg, Pennsylvania 18360

Phone: 1-570-476-8006
Fax: 1-570-476-0860

acl@aclweb.org

Additional copies of this publication are available from:

Curran Associates, Inc.
57 Morehouse Lane
Red Hook, NY 12571 USA
Phone: 845-758-0400
Fax: 845-758-2634
Email: curran@proceedings.com
Web: www.proceedings.com

Introduction

NLP researchers are now building educational applications across a number of areas, including automated evaluation of student writing and speaking, rich grammatical error detection with an increasing focus on English language learning, tools to support student reading, and intelligent tutoring.

This workshop is the fourth in a series, specifically related to "Building NLP Applications for Education", that began at NAACL/HLT (2003), and continued at ACL 2005 (Ann Arbor), ACL-HLT 2008 (Columbus), and now, at NAACL-HLT 2009 (Boulder). Research in this area continues to grow, and there is ever-increasing interest which was evidenced this year by the fact that we had the largest number of submissions.

For this workshop, we received 25 submissions and accepted 12 papers. All of these papers are published in these proceedings. Each paper was reviewed by a least two members of the Program Committee.

The papers in this workshop fall under several main themes:

- **Assessing Speech -** Two papers deal with assessing spoken language [Zechner et al] and [Cheng et al];
- **Grammar Error Detection -** The majority of papers this year deal with grammar error detection for native and non-native English speakers [Liu et al], [Tsao and Wible], [Leacock et al], [Hermet and Alain], and [Foster and Andersen].
- **Reading Support -** Two papers support vocabulary building [Pino and Eskenazi] and [Landauer et al], and another paper discusses a literacy aid for Brazilian Portuguese [Candido et al].
- **Intelligent Tutoring -** Two papers discuss issues concerning intelligent tutoring systems [Boyer et al] and [Kersey et al].

We wish to thank everyone who showed interest and submitted a paper, all of the authors for their contributions, the members of the Program Committee for their thoughtful reviews, and everyone who attended this workshop. All of these factors contribute to a truly rich and successful event!

Joel Tetreault, Educational Testing Service
Jill Burstein, Educational Testing Service
Claudia Leacock, Butler Hill Group

Organizers:

Joel Tetreault, Educational Testing Service
Jill Burstein, Educational Testing Service
Claudia Leacock, Butler Hill Group

Program Committee:

Martin Chodorow, Hunter College, CUNY, USA
Bill Dolan, Microsoft, USA
Jennifer Foster, Dublin City University, Ireland
Michael Gamon, Microsoft, USA
Maxine Eskenazi, Carnegie Mellon University, USA
Na-Rae Han, Korea University, Korea
Trude Heift, Simon Frasier University, Canada
Derrick Higgins, ETS, USA
Emi Izumi, NICT, Japan
Ola Knutsson, KTH Nada, Sweden
John Lee, MIT, USA
Diane Litman, University of Pittsburgh, USA
Detmar Meurers, University of Tubingen, Germany
Lisa Michaud, Saint Anselm College, USA
Ani Nenkova, University of Pennsylvania, USA
Ted Pedersen, University of Minnesota, USA
Mihai Rotaru, TextKernel, the Netherlands
Mathias Schulze, University of Waterloo, Canada
Stephanie Seneff, MIT, USA
Richard Sproat, Oregon Graduate Institute, USA
Jana Sukkarieh, ETS, USA
Svetlana Stenchikova, Stony Brook University, USA
David Wible, National Central University, Taiwan

Table of Contents

Conference Program

Friday, June 5, 2009

9:00–9:15 Opening Remarks

9:15–9:40 *Automated Assessment of Spoken Modern Standard Arabic*
Jian Cheng, Jared Bernstein, Ulrike Pado and Masanori Suzuki

9:40–10:05 *Automatic Scoring of Children's Read-Aloud Text Passages and Word Lists*
Klaus Zechner, John Sabatini and Lei Chen

10:05–10:30 *Inferring Tutorial Dialogue Structure with Hidden Markov Modeling*
Kristy Elizabeth Boyer, Eun Young Ha, Robert Phillips, Michael Wallis, Mladen Vouk and James Lester

10:30–11:00 Break

11:00–11:25 *A New Yardstick and Tool for Personalized Vocabulary Building*
Thomas Landauer, Kirill Kireyev and Charles Panaccione

11:25–11:50 *Supporting the Adaptation of Texts for Poor Literacy Readers: a Text Simplification Editor for Brazilian Portuguese*
Arnaldo Candido, Erick Maziero, Lucia Specia, Caroline Gasperin, Thiago Pardo and Sandra Aluisio

11:50–12:15 *An Application of Latent Semantic Analysis to Word Sense Discrimination for Words with Related and Unrelated Meanings*
Juan Pino and Maxine Eskenazi

12:15–2:15 Lunch

2:15–2:40 *Automated Suggestions for Miscollocations*
Anne Li-E Liu, David Wible and Nai-Lung Tsao

2:40–3:05 *A Method for Unsupervised Broad-Coverage Lexical Error Detection and Correction*
Nai-Lung Tsao and David Wible

3:05–3:30 *KSC-PaL: A Peer Learning Agent that Encourages Students to take the Initiative*
Cynthia Kersey, Barbara Di Eugenio, Pamela Jordan and Sandra Katz

3:30–4:00 Break

Friday, June 5, 2009 (continued)

4:00–4:25 *Using First and Second Language Models to Correct Preposition Errors in Second Language Authoring*
Matthieu Hermet and Désilets Alain

4:25–4:50 *User Input and Interactions on Microsoft Research ESL Assistant*
Claudia Leacock, Michael Gamon and Chris Brockett

4:50–5:15 *GenERRate: Generating Errors for Use in Grammatical Error Detection*
Jennifer Foster and Oistein Andersen

Automatic Assessment of Spoken Modern Standard Arabic

Jian Cheng, Jared Bernstein, Ulrike Pado, Masanori Suzuki
Pearson Knowledge Technologies
299 California Ave, Palo Alto, CA 94306
jian.cheng@pearson.com

Abstract

Proficiency testing is an important ingredient in successful language teaching. However, repeated testing for course placement, over the course of instruction or for certification can be time-consuming and costly. We present the design and validation of the Versant Arabic Test, a fully automated test of spoken Modern Standard Arabic, that evaluates test-takers' facility in listening and speaking. Experimental data shows the test to be highly reliable (test-retest r=0.97) and to strongly predict performance on the ILR OPI (r=0.87), a standard interview test that assesses oral proficiency.

1 Introduction

Traditional high-stakes testing of spoken proficiency often evaluates the test-taker's ability to accomplish communicative tasks in a conversational setting. For example, learners may introduce themselves, respond to requests for information, or accomplish daily tasks in a role-play.

Testing oral proficiency in this way can be time-consuming and costly, since at least one trained interviewer is needed for each student. For example, the standard oral proficiency test used by the United States government agencies (the Interagency Language Roundtable Oral Proficiency Interview or ILR OPI) is usually administered by two certified interviewers for approximately 30-45 minutes per candidate.

The great effort involved in oral proficiency interview (OPI) testing makes automated testing an attractive alternative. Work has been reported on fully automated scoring of speaking ability (e.g., Bernstein & Barbier, 2001; Zechner et al., 2007, for English; Balogh & Bernstein, 2007, for English and Spanish). Automated testing systems do not aim to simulate a conversation with the test-taker and therefore do not directly observe interactive human communication. Bernstein and Barbier (2001) describe a system that might be used in qualifying simultaneous interpreters; Zechner et al. (2007) describe an automated scoring system that assesses performance according to the TOEFL iBT speaking rubrics. Balogh and Bernstein (2007) focus on evaluating *facility* in a spoken language, a separate test construct that relates to oral proficiency.

"Facility in a spoken language" is defined as "the ability to understand a spoken language on everyday topics and to respond appropriately and intelligibly at a native-like conversational pace" (Balogh & Bernstein, 2007, p. 272). This ability is assumed to underlie high performance in communicative settings, since learners have to understand their interlocutors correctly and efficiently in real time to be able to respond. Equally, learners have to be able to formulate and articulate a comprehensible answer without undue delay. Testing for *oral proficiency*, on the other hand, conventionally includes additional aspects such as correct interpretation of the pragmatics of the conversation, socially and culturally appropriate wording and content and knowledge of the subject matter under discussion.

In this paper, we describe the design and validation of the Versant Arabic Test (VAT), a fully automated test of facility with spoken Modern Standard Arabic (MSA). Focusing on facility rather than communication-based oral proficiency enables the creation of an efficient yet informative automated test of listening and speaking ability. The automated test can be administered over the telephone or on a computer in approximately 17 minutes. Despite its much shorter format and constrained tasks, test-taker scores on the VAT

Proceedings of the NAACL HLT Workshop on Innovative Use of NLP for Building Educational Applications, pages 1–9,
Boulder, Colorado, June 2009.

strongly correspond to their scores from an ILR Oral Proficiency Interview.

The paper is structured as follows: After reviewing related work, we describe Modern Standard Arabic and introduce the test construct (i.e., what the test is intended to measure) in detail (Section 3). We then describe the structure and development of the VAT in Section 4 and present evidence for its reliability and validity in Section 5.

2 Related Work

The use of automatic speech recognition appeared earliest in pronunciation tutoring systems in the field of language learning. Examples include SRI's AUTOGRADER (Bernstein et al., 1990), the CMU FLUENCY system (Eskenazi, 1996; Eskenazi & Hansma, 1998) and SRI's commercial EduSpeak system (Franco et al., 2000). In such systems, learner speech is typically evaluated by comparing features like phone duration, spectral characteristics of phones and rate-of-speech to a model of native speaker performances. Systems evaluate learners' pronunciation and give some feedback.

Automated measurement of more comprehensive speaking and listening ability was first reported by Townshend et al. (1998), describing the early PhonePass test development at Ordinate. The PhonePass tests returned five diagnostic scores, including reading fluency, repeat fluency and listening vocabulary. Ordinate's Spoken Spanish Test also included automatically scored passage retellings that used an adapted form of latent semantic analysis to estimate vocabulary scores.

More recently at ETS, Zechner et al. (2007) describe experiments in automatic scoring of test-taker responses in a TOEFL iBT practice environment, focusing mostly on fluency features. Zechner and Xi (2008) report work on similar algorithms to score item types with varying degrees of response predictability, including items with a very restricted range of possible answers (e.g., reading aloud) as well as item types with progressively less restricted answers (e.g., describing a picture – relatively predictable, or stating an opinion – less predictable). The scoring mechanism in Zechner and Xi (2008) employs features such as the average number of word types or silences for fluency estimation, the ASR HMM log-likelihood for pronunciation or a vector-based similarity measure to assess vocabulary and content. Zechner and Xi present correlations of machine scores with human scores for two tasks: r=0.50 for an opinion task and r=0.69 for picture description, which are comparable to the modest human rater agreement figures in this data.

Balogh and Bernstein (2007) describe operational automated tests of spoken Spanish and English that return an overall ability score and four diagnostic subscores (sentence mastery, vocabulary, fluency, pronunciation). The tests measure a learner's facility in listening to and speaking a foreign language. The facility construct can be tested by observing performance on many kinds of tasks that elicit responses in real time with varying, but generally high, predictability. More predictable items have two important advantages: As with domain restricted speech recognition tasks in general, the recognition of response content is more accurate, but a higher precision scoring system is also possible as an independent effect beyond the greater recognition accuracy. Scoring is based on features like word stress, segmental form, latency or rate of speaking for the fluency and pronunciation subscores, and on response fidelity with expected responses for the two content subscores. Balogh and Bernstein report that their tests are highly reliable (r>0.95 for both English and Spanish) and that test scores strongly predict human ratings of oral proficiency based on Common European Framework of Reference language ability descriptors (r=0.88 English, r=0.90 Spanish).

3 Versant Arabic Test: Facility in Modern Standard Arabic

We describe a fully operational test of spoken MSA that follows the tests described in Balogh and Bernstein (2007) in structure and method, and in using the facility construct. There are two important dimensions to the test's construct: One is the definition of what comprises MSA, and the other the definition of facility.

3.1 Target Language: Modern Standard Arabic

Modern Standard Arabic is a non-colloquial language used throughout the Arabic-speaking world for writing and in spoken communication within public, literary, and educational settings. It differs from the colloquial dialects of Arabic that are spoken in the countries of North Africa and the Middle East in lexicon and in syntax, for example in the use of explicit case and mood marking.

Written MSA can be identified by its specific syntactic style and lexical forms. However, since all short vowels are omitted in normal printed material, the word-final short vowels indicating case and mood are provided by the speaker, even when reading MSA aloud. This means that a text that is syntactically and lexically MSA can be read in a way that exhibits features of the regional dialect of the speaker if case and mood vowels are omitted or phonemes are realized in regional pronunciations. Also, a speaker's dialectal and educational background may influence the choice of lexical items and syntactic structures in spontaneous speech. The MSA spoken on radio and television in the Arab world therefore shows a significant variation of syntax, phonology, and lexicon.

3.2 Facility

We define *facility* in spoken MSA as the ability to understand and speak contemporary MSA as it is used in international communication for broadcast, for commerce, and for professional collaboration. Listening and speaking skills are assessed by observing test-taker performance on spoken tasks that demand understanding a spoken prompt, and formulating and articulating a response in real time.

Success on the real-time language tasks depends on whether the test-taker can process spoken material efficiently. Automaticity is an important underlying factor in such efficient language processing (Cutler, 2003). Automaticity is the ability to access and retrieve lexical items, to build phrases and clause structures, and to articulate responses without conscious attention to the linguistic code (Cutler, 2003; Jescheniak et al., 2003; Levelt, 2001). If processing is automatic, the listener/speaker can focus on the communicative content rather than on how the language code is structured. Latency and pace of the spoken response can be seen as partial manifestation of the test-taker's automaticity.

Unlike the oral proficiency construct that coordinates with the structure and scoring of OPI tests, the facility construct does not extend to social skills, higher cognitive functions (e.g., persuasion), or world knowledge. However, we show below that test scores for language facility predict almost all of the reliable variance in test scores for an interview-based test of language and communication.

4 Versant Arabic Test

The VAT consists of five tasks with a total of 69 items. Four diagnostic subscores as well as an overall score are returned. Test administration and scoring is fully automated and utilizes speech processing technology to estimate features of the speech signal and extract response content.

4.1 Test Design

The VAT items were designed to represent core syntactic constructions of MSA and probe a wide range of ability levels. To make sure that the VAT items used realistic language structures, texts were adapted from spontaneous spoken utterances found in international televised broadcasts with the vocabulary altered to contain common words that a learner of Arabic may have encountered.

Four educated native Arabic speakers wrote the items and five dialectically distinct native Arabic speakers (Arabic linguist/teachers) independently reviewed the items for correctness and appropriateness of content. Finally, fifteen educated native Arabic speakers (eight men and seven women) from seven different countries recorded the vetted items at a conversational pace, providing a range of native accents and MSA speaking styles in the item prompts.

4.2 Test Tasks and Structure

The VAT has five task types that are arranged in six sections (Parts A through F): Readings, Repeats (presented in two sections), Short Answer Questions, Sentence Builds, and Passage Retellings. These item types provide multiple, fully independent measures that underlie facility with spoken MSA, including phonological fluency, sentence construction and comprehension, passive and active vocabulary use, and pronunciation of rhythmic and segmental units.

Part A: Reading (6 items) In this task, test-takers read six (out of eight) printed sentences, one at a time, in the order requested by the examiner voice. Reading items are printed in Arabic script with short vowels indicated as they would be in a basal school reader. Test-takers have the opportunity to familiarize themselves with the reading items before the test begins. The sentences are relatively simple in structure and vocabulary, so they can be read easily and fluently by people educated in MSA. For test-takers with little facility in spoken Arabic but with some reading skills, this task provides samples of pronunciation and oral reading fluency.

Parts B and E: Repeats (2x15 items) Test-takers hear sentences and are asked to repeat them verbatim. The sentences were recorded by native speakers of Arabic at a conversational pace. Sentences range in length from three words to at most twelve words, although few items are longer than nine words. To repeat a sentence longer than about seven syllables, the test-taker has to recognize the words as produced in a continuous stream of speech (Miller & Isard, 1963). Generally, the ability to repeat material is constrained by the size of the linguistic unit that a person can process in an automatic or nearly automatic fashion. The ability to repeat longer and longer items indicates more and more advanced language skills – particularly automaticity with phrase and clause structures.

Part C: Short Answer Questions (20 items) Test-takers listen to spoken questions in MSA and answer each question with a single word or short phrase. Each question asks for basic information or requires simple inferences based on time, sequence, number, lexical content, or logic. The questions are designed not to presume any specialist knowledge of specific facts of Arabic culture or other subject matter. An English example[1] of a Short Answer Question would be "*Do you get milk from a bottle or a newspaper?*" To answer the questions, the test-taker needs to identify the words in phonological and syntactic context, infer the demand proposition and formulate the answer.

Part D: Sentence Building (10 items) Test-takers are presented with three short phrases. The phrases are presented in a random order (excluding the original, naturally occurring phrase order), and the test-taker is asked to respond with a reasonable sentence that comprises exactly the three given phrases. An English example would be a prompt of "*was reading - my mother - her favorite magazine*", with the correct response: "*My mother was reading her favorite magazine.*" In this task, the test-taker has to understand the possible meanings of each phrase and know how the phrases might be combined with the other phrasal material, both with regard to syntax and semantics. The length and complexity of the sentence that can be built is constrained by the size of the linguistic units with which the test-taker represents the prompt phrases in verbal working memory (e.g., a syllable, a word or a multi-word phrase).

Part F: Passage Retelling (3 items) In this final task, test-takers listen to a spoken passage (usually a story) and then are asked to retell the passage in their own words. Test-takers are encouraged to retell as much of the passage as they can, including the situation, characters, actions and ending. The passages are from 19 to 50 words long. Passage Retellings require listening comprehension of extended speech and also provide additional samples of spontaneous speech. Currently, this task is not automatically scored in this test.

4.3 Test Administration

Administration of the test takes about 17 minutes and the test can be taken over the phone or via a computer. A single examiner voice presents all the spoken instructions in either English or Arabic and all the spoken instructions are also printed verbatim on a test paper or displayed on the computer screen. Test items are presented in Arabic by native speaker voices that are distinct from the examiner voice. Each test administration contains 69 items selected by a stratified random draw from a large item pool. Scores are available online within a few minutes after the test is completed.

4.4 Scoring Dimensions

The VAT provides four diagnostic subscores that indicate the test-taker's ability profile over various dimensions of facility with spoken MSA. The subscores are

- *Sentence Mastery*: Understanding, recalling, and producing MSA phrases and clauses in complete sentences.
- *Vocabulary*: Understanding common words spoken in continuous sentence context and producing such words as needed.
- *Fluency*: Appropriate rhythm, phrasing and timing when constructing, reading and repeating sentences.
- *Pronunciation*: Producing consonants, vowels, and lexical stress in a native-like manner in sentence context.

[1] See Pearson (2009) for Arabic example items.

The VAT also reports an Overall score, which is a weighted average of the four subscores (Sentence Mastery contributes 30%, Vocabulary 20%, Fluency 30%, and Pronunciation 20%).

4.5 Automated Scoring

The VAT's automated scoring system was trained on native and non-native responses to the test items as well as human ability judgments.

Data Collection For the development of the VAT, a total of 246 hours of speech in response to the test items was collected from natives and learners and was transcribed by educated native speakers of Arabic. Subsets of the response data were also rated for proficiency. Three trained native speakers produced about 7,500 judgments for each of the Fluency and the Pronunciation subscores (on a scale from 1-6, with 0 indicating missing data). The raters agreed well with one another at $r \approx 0.8$ ($r=0.79$ for Pronunciation, $r=0.83$ for Fluency). All test administrations included in the concurrent validation study (cf. Section 5 below) were excluded from the training of the scoring system.

Automatic Speech Recognition Recognition is performed by an HMM-based recognizer built using the HTK toolkit (Young et al., 2000). Three-state triphone acoustic models were trained on 130 hours of non-native and 116 hours of native MSA speech. The expected response networks for each item were induced from the transcriptions of native and non-native responses.

Since standard written Arabic does not mark short vowels, the pronunciation and meaning of written words is often ambiguous and words do not show case and mood markings. This is a challenge to Arabic ASR, since it complicates the creation of pronunciation dictionaries that link a word's sound to its written form. Words were represented with their fully voweled pronunciation (cf., Vergyri et al., 2008; Soltau et al., 2007). We relied on hand-corrected automatic diacritization of the standard written transcriptions to create fully-voweled words from which phonemic representations were automatically created.

The orthographic transcript of a test-taker utterance in standard, unvoweled form is still ambiguous with regard to the actual words uttered, since the same consonant string can have different meanings depending on the vowels that are inserted. Moreover, the different words written in this way are usually semantically related, making them potentially confusable for language learners. Therefore, for system development, we transcribed words with full vowel marks whenever a vowel change would cause a change of meaning. This partial voweling procedure deviates from the standard way of writing, but it facilitated system-internal comparison of target answers with observed test-taker utterances since the target pronunciation was made explicit.

Scoring Methods The Sentence Mastery and Vocabulary scores are derived from the accuracy of the test-taker's response (in terms of number of words inserted, deleted, or substituted by the candidate), and the presence or absence of expected words in correct sequences, respectively.

The Fluency and Pronunciation subscores are calculated by measuring the latency of the response, the rate of speaking, the position and length of pauses, the stress and segmental forms of the words, and the pronunciation of the segments in the words within their lexical and phrasal context. The final subscores are based on a non-linear combination of these features. The non-linear model is trained on feature values and human judgments for native and non-native speech.

Figure 1 shows how each subscore draws on responses from the different task types to yield a stable estimate of test-taker ability. The Pronunciation score is estimated from responses to Reading, Repeat and Sentence Build items. The Fluency score uses the same set of responses as for Pronunciation, but a different set of acoustic features are extracted and combined in the score. Sentence Mastery is derived from Repeat and Sentence Building items and Vocabulary is based on responses to the Short Answer Questions.

5 Evaluation

For any test to be meaningful, two properties are crucial: *Reliability* and *validity*. Reliability represents how consistent and replicable the test scores are. Validity represents the extent to which one can justify making certain inferences or decisions on the basis of test scores. Reliability is a necessary condition for validity, since inconsistent measurements cannot support inferences that would justify real-world decision making.

To investigate the reliability and the validity of the VAT, a concurrent validation study was conducted in which a group of test-takers took both

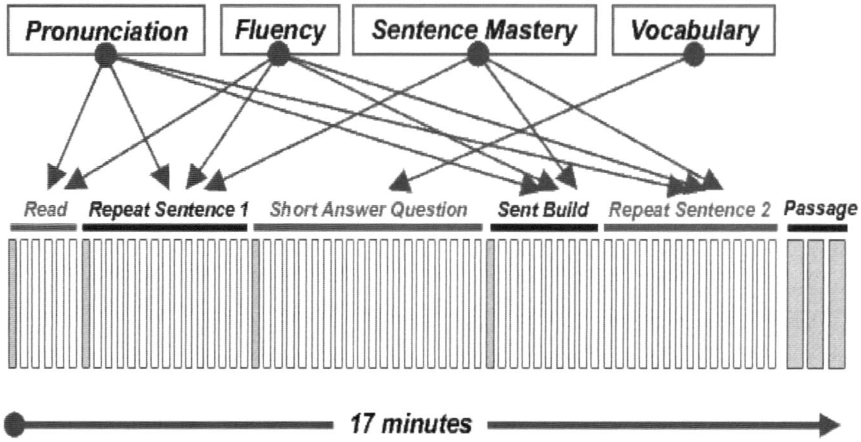

Figure 1: Relation of subscores to item types.

the VAT and the ILR OPI. If the VAT scores are comparable to scores from a reliable traditional measure of oral proficiency in MSA, this will be a piece of evidence that the VAT indeed captures important aspects of test-takers' abilities in using spoken MSA.

As additional evidence to establish the validity of the VAT, we examined the performance of the native and non-native speaker groups. Since the test claims to measure facility in understanding and speaking MSA, most educated native speakers should do quite well on the test, whereas the scores of the non-native test-takers should spread out according to their ability level. Furthermore, one would also expect that educated native speakers would perform equally well regardless of specific national dialect backgrounds and no important score differences among different national groups of educated native speakers should be observed.

5.1 Concurrent Validation Study

ILR OPIs. The ILR Oral Proficiency Interview is a well-established test of spoken language performance, and serves as the standard evaluation tool used by United States government agencies (see www.govtilr.org). The test is a structured interview that elicits spoken performances that are graded according to the ILR skill levels. These levels describe the test-taker's ability in terms of communicative functioning in the target language. The OPI test construct is therefore different from that of the VAT, which measures facility with spoken Arabic, and not communicative ability, as such.

Concurrent Sample. A total of 118 test-takers (112 non-natives and six Arabic natives) took two VATs and two ILR OPIs. Each test-taker completed all four tests within a 15 day window. The mean age of the test-takers was 27 years old (SD = 7) and the male-to-female split was 60-to-58. Of the non-native speakers in this concurrent testing sample, at least 20 test-takers were learning Arabic at a college in the U.S., and at least 11 were graduates from the Center for Arabic Studies Abroad program. Nine test-takers were recruited at a language school in Cairo, Egypt, and the remainder were current or former students of Arabic recruited in the US.

Seven active government-certified oral proficiency interviewers conducted the ILR OPIs over the telephone. Each OPI was administered by two interviewers who submitted the performance ratings independently after each interview. The average inter-rater correlation between one rater and the average score given by the other two raters administering the same test-taker's other interview was 0.90.

The test scores used in the concurrent study are the VAT Overall score, reported here in a range from 10 to 90, and the ILR OPI scores with levels {0, 0+, 1, 1+, 2, 2+, 3, 3+, 4, 4+, 5}[2].

5.2 Reliability

Since each test-taker took the VAT twice, we can estimate the VAT's reliability using the test-retest method (e.g., Crocker & Algina, 1986: 133). The

[2] All plus ratings (e.g., 1+, 2+, etc) were converted with 0.5 (e.g, 1.5, 2.5, etc) in the analysis reported in this paper.

correlation between the scores from the first administration and the scores from the second administration was found to be at r=0.97, indicating high reliability of the VAT test. The scores from one test administration explain 0.97^2=94% of the score variance in another test administration to the same group of test-takers.

We also compute the reliability of the ILR OPI scores for each test taker by correlating the averages of the ratings for each of the two test administrations. The OPI scores are reliable at r=0.91 (thus 83% of the variance in the test scores are shared by the scores of another administration). This indicates that the OPI procedure implemented in the validation study was relatively consistent.

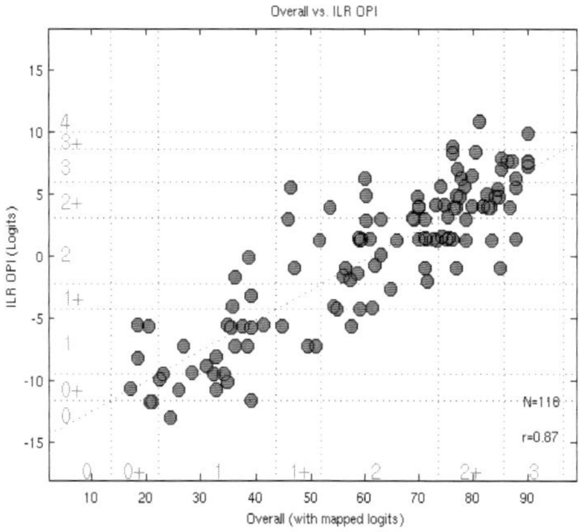

Figure 2: Test-takers' ILR OPI scores as a function of VAT scores (r=0.87; N=118).

5.3 Validity

Evidence here for VAT score validity comes from two sources: the prediction of ILR OPI scores (assumed for now to be valid) and the performance distribution of native and non-native test takers.

Prediction of ILR OPI Test Scores. For the comparison of the VAT to the ILR OPI, a scaled average OPI score was computed for each test-taker from all the available ILR OPI ratings. The scaling was performed using a computer program, FACETS, which takes into account rater severity and test-taker ability and therefore produces a fairer estimate than a simple average (Linacre et al., 1990; Linacre, 2003).

Figure 2 is a scatterplot of the ILR OPI scores and VAT scores for the concurrent validation sample (N=118). IRT scaling of the ILR scores allows a mapping of the scaled OPI scores and the VAT scores onto the original OPI levels, which are given on the inside of the plot axes. The correlation coefficient of the two test scores is r=0.87. This is roughly in the same range as both the ILR OPI reliability and the average ILR OPI inter-rater correlation. The test scores on the VAT account for 76% of the variation in the ILR OPI scores (in contrast to 83% accounted for by another ILR OPI test administration and 81% accounted for by one other ILR OPI interviewer).

The VAT accounts for most of the variance in the interview-based test of oral proficiency in MSA. This is one form of confirming evidence that the VAT captures important aspects of MSA speaking and listening ability.

The close correspondence of the VAT scores with ILR OPI scores, despite the difference in construct, may come about because candidates easily transfer basic social and communicative skills acquired in their native language, as long as they are able to correctly and efficiently process (i.e., comprehend and produce) the second language. Also, highly proficient learners have most likely acquired their skills at least to some extent in social interaction with native speakers of their second language and therefore know how to interact appropriately.

Group Performance. Finally, we examine the score distributions for different groups of test-takers to investigate whether three basic expectations are met:

- Native speakers all perform well, while non-natives show a range of ability levels
- Non-native speakers spread widely across the scoring scale (the test can distinguish well between a range of non-native ability levels)
- Native speakers from different countries perform similarly (national origin does not predict native performance)

We compare the score distributions of test-taker groups in the training data set, which contains 1309 native and 1337 non-native tests. For each test in the data set, an Overall score is computed by the trained scoring system on the basis of the recorded responses. Figure 3 presents cumulative distribution functions of the VAT overall scores, showing for each score which percentage of test-takers performs at or below that level. This figure compares two speaker groups: Educated native speakers of Arabic and learners of Arabic. The

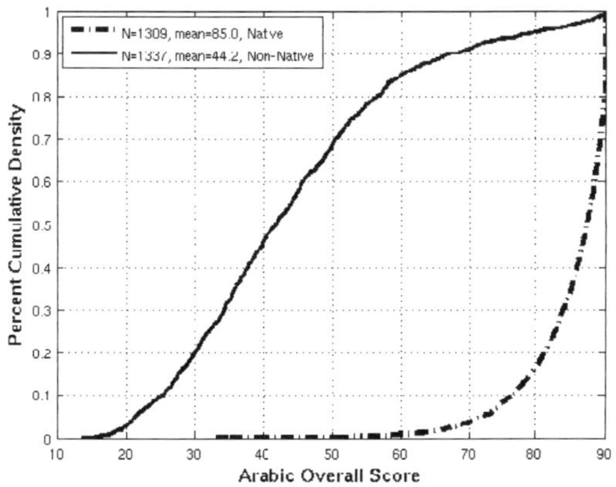

Figure 3: Score distributions for native and non-native speakers.

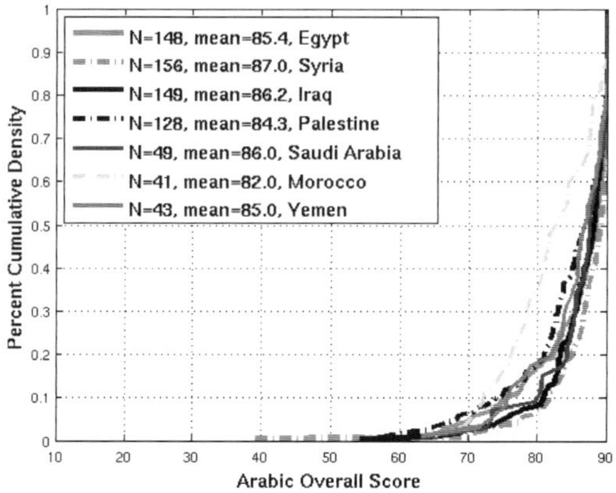

Figure 4: Score distributions for native speakers of different countries of origin.

score distributions of the native speakers and the learner sample are clearly different. For example, fewer than 5% of the native speakers score below 70, while fewer than 10% of the learners score above 70. Further, the shape of the learner curve indicates a wide distribution of scores, suggesting that the VAT discriminates well in the range of abilities of learners of Arabic as a foreign language.

Figure 4 is also a cumulative distribution functions, but it shows score distributions for native speakers by country of origin (showing only countries with at least 40 test-takers). The curves for Egyptian, Syrian, Iraqi, Palestinian, Saudi and Yemeni speakers are indistinguishable. The Moroccan speakers are slightly separate from the other native speakers, but only a negligible number of them scores lower than 70, a score that less than 10% of learners achieve. This finding supports the notion that the VAT scores reflect a speaker's facility in spoken MSA, irrespective of the speaker's country of origin.

6 Conclusion

We have presented an automatically scored test of facility with spoken Modern Standard Arabic (MSA). The test yields an ability profile over four subscores, Fluency and Pronunciation (manner-of-speaking) as well as Sentence Mastery and Vocabulary (content), and generates a single Overall score as the weighted average of the subscores. We have presented data from a validation study with native and non-native test-takers that shows the VAT to be highly reliable (test-retest r=0.97). We also have presented validity evidence for justifying the use of VAT scores as a measure of oral proficiency in MSA. While educated native speakers of Arabic can score high on the test regardless of their country of origin because they all possess high facility in spoken MSA, learners of Arabic score differently according to their ability levels; the VAT test scores account for most of the variance in the interview-based ILR OPI for MSA, indicating that the VAT captures a major feature of oral proficiency.

In summary, the empirical validation data suggests that the VAT can be an efficient, practical alternative to interview-based proficiency testing in many settings, and that VAT scores can be used to inform decisions in which a person's listening and speaking ability in Modern Standard Arabic should play a part.

Acknowledgments

The reported work was conducted under contract W912SU-06-P-0041 from the U.S. Dept. of the Army. The authors thank Andy Freeman for providing diacritic markings, and to Waheed Samy, Naima Bousofara Omar, Eli Andrews, Mohamed Al-Saffar, Nazir Kikhia, Rula Kikhia, and Linda Istanbulli for support with item development and data collection/transcription in Arabic.

References

Jennifer Balogh and Jared Bernstein. 2007. Workable models of standard performance in English and Spanish. In Y. Matsumoto, D. Oshima, O. Robinson, and P. Sells, editors, *Diversity in Language: Perspectives and Implications* (CSLI Lecture Notes, 176), 271-292. CSLI, Stanford, CA.

Jared Bernstein and Isabella Barbier. 2001. Design and development parameters for a rapid automatic screening test for prospective simultaneous interpreters. *Interpreting, International Journal of Research and Practice in Interpreting*, 5(2): 221-238.

Jared Bernstein, Michael Cohen, Hy Murveit, Dmitry Rtischev, and Mitch Weintraub. 1990. Automatic evaluation and training in English pronunciation. In *Proceedings of ICSLP*, 1185-1188.

Linda Crocker and James Algina. 1986. *Introduction to Classical & Modern Test Theory*. Harcourt Brace Jovanovich, Orland, FL.

Anne Cutler. 2003. Lexical access. In L. Nadel, editor, *Encyclopedia of Cognitive Science*, volume 2, pp. 858-864. Nature Publishing Group.

Maxine Eskenazi. 1996. Detection of foreign speakers' pronunciation errors for second language training – preliminary results. In *Proceedings of ICSLP '96*.

Maxine Eskenazi and Scott Hansma. 1998. The fluency pronunciation trainer. In *Proceedings of the STiLL Workshop*.

Horacio Franco, Victor Abrash, Kristin Precoda, Harry Bratt, Raman Rao, John Butzberger, Romain Rossier, and Federico Cesar. 2000. The SRI EduSpeak system: Recognition and pronunciation scoring for language learning. In *Proceedings of InSTiLL*, 123-128.

Jörg Jescheniak, Anja Hahne, and Herbert Schriefers. 2003. Information flow in the mental lexicon during speech planning: Evidence from event-related potentials. *Cognitive Brain Research*, 15(3):858-864.

Willem Levelt. 2001. Spoken word production: A theory of lexical access. *Proceedings of the National Academy of Sciences*, 98(23):13464-13471.

John Linacre. 2003. *FACETS Rasch measurement computer program*. Winstep, Chicago, IL.

John Linacre, Benjamin Wright, and Mary Lunz. 1990. A Facets model for judgmental scoring. *Memo 61*. MESA Psychometric Laboratory. University of Chicago. Retrieved April 14, 2009, from http:// http://www.rasch.org/memo61.htm.

George Miller and Stephen Isard. 1963. Some perceptual consequences of linguistic rules. *Journal of Verbal Learning and Verbal Behavior*, 2:217-228.

Pearson. 2009. *Versant Arabic test – test description and validation summary*. Pearson. Retrieved April 14, 2009, from http://www.ordinate.com/technology/VersantArabicTestValidation.pdf.

Hagen Soltau, George Saon, Daniel Povy, Lidia Mangu, Brian Kingsbury, Jeff Kuo, Mohamed Omar, and Geoffrey Zweig. 2007. The IBM 2006 GALE Arabic ASR system. In *Proceedings of ICASSP 2007*, 349-352.

Brent Townshend, Jared Bernstein, Ognjen Todic & Eryk Warren. 1998. Estimation of Spoken Language Proficiency. In *STiLL: Speech Technology in Language Learning*, 177-180.

Dimitra Vergyri, Arindam Mandal, Wen Wang, Andreas Stolcke, Jing Zheng, Martin Graciarena, David Rybach, Christian Gollan, Ralf Schlüter, Karin Kirchhoff, Arlo Faria, and Nelson Morgan. 2008. Development of the SRI/Nightingale Arabic ASR system. In *Proceedings of Interspeech 2008*, 1437-1440.

Steve Young, Dan Kershaw, Julian Odell, Dave Ollason, Valtcho Valtchev, and Phil Woodland. 2000. *The HTK Book Version 3.0*. Cambridge University Press, Cambridge, UK.

Klaus Zechner and Xiaoming Xi. 2008. Towards automatic scoring of a test of spoken language with heterogeneous task types. In *Proceedings of the Third Workshop on Innovative Use of NLP for Building Educational Applications*, 98-106.

Klaus Zechner, Derrick Higgins, and Xiaoming Xi. 2007. SpeechRater™: A construct-driven approach to score spontaneous non-native speech. In *Proceedings of the Workshop of the ISCA SIG on Speech and Language Technology in Education*.

Automatic Scoring of Children's Read-Aloud Text Passages and Word Lists

Klaus Zechner and **John Sabatini** and **Lei Chen**
Educational Testing Service
Rosedale Road
Princeton, NJ 08541, USA
{kzechner,jsabatini,lchen}@ets.org

Abstract

Assessment of reading proficiency is typically done by asking subjects to read a text passage silently and then answer questions related to the text. An alternate approach, measuring reading-aloud proficiency, has been shown to correlate well with the aforementioned common method and is used as a paradigm in this paper.

We describe a system that is able to automatically score two types of children's read speech samples (text passages and word lists), using automatic speech recognition and the target criterion "correctly read words per minute". Its performance is dependent on the data type (passages vs. word lists) as well as on the relative difficulty of passages or words for individual readers. Pearson correlations with human assigned scores are around 0.86 for passages and around 0.80 for word lists.

1 Introduction

It has long been noted that a substantial number of U.S. students in the 10-14 years age group have deficiencies in their reading competence (National Center of Educational Statistics, 2006). With the enactment of the No Child Left Behind Act (2002), interest and focus on objectively assessing and improving this unsatisfactory situation has come to the forefront.

While assessment of reading is usually done post-hoc with measures of reading comprehension, direct reading assessment is also often performed using a different method, oral (read-aloud) reading. In this paradigm, students read texts aloud and their proficiency in terms of speed, fluency, pronunciation, intonation etc. can be monitored directly while reading is in progress. In the reading research literature, oral reading has been one of the best diagnostic and predictive measures of foundational reading weaknesses and of overall reading ability (e.g., Deno et al., 2001; Wayman et al., 2007). An association between low reading comprehension and slow, inaccurate reading rate has been confirmed repeatedly in middle school populations (e.g., Deno & Marsten, 2006). Correlations consistently fall in the 0.65-0.7 range for predicting untimed passage reading comprehension test outcomes (Wayman et al., 2007).

In this paper, we investigate the feasibility of large-scale, automatic assessment of read-aloud speech of middle school students with a reasonable degree of accuracy (these students typically attend grades 6-8 and their age is in the 10-14 years range). If possible, this would improve the utility of oral reading as a large-scale, school-based assessment technique, making it more efficient by saving costs and time of human annotations and grading of reading errors.

The most widely used measure of oral reading proficiency is "correctly read words per minute" (cwpm) (Wayman et al., 2007). To obtain this measure, students' read speech samples are first

Proceedings of the NAACL HLT Workshop on Innovative Use of NLP for Building Educational Applications, pages 10–18,
Boulder, Colorado, June 2009.

recorded, then the reading time is determined, and finally a human rater has to listen to the recording and note all reading errors and sum them up. Reading errors are categorized into word substitutions, deletions etc.

We have several sets of digitally recorded read-aloud samples from middle school students available which were not collected for use with automatic speech recognition (ASR) but which were scored by hand.

Our approach here is to pass the children's speech samples through an automatic speech recognizer and then to align its output word hypotheses with the original text that was read by the student. From this alignment and from the reading time, an estimate for the above mentioned measure of cwpm can then be computed. If the automatically computed cwpm measures are close enough to those obtained by human hand-scoring, this process may be employed in real world settings eventually to save much time and money.

Recognizing children's speech, however, has been shown to be substantially harder than adult speech (Lee et al., 1999; Li and Russell, 2002), which is partly due to children's higher degree of variability in different dimensions of language such as pronunciation or grammar. In our data, there was also a substantial number of non-native speakers of English, presenting additional challenges. We used targeted training and adaptation of our ASR systems to achieve reasonable word accuracies. While for text passages, the word accuracy on unseen speakers was about 72%, it was only about 50% for word lists, which was due in part to a higher percentage of non-native speakers in this data set, to the fact that various sources of noise often prevented the recognizer from correctly locating the spoken words in the signal, and also due to our choice of a uniform language model since conventional n-gram models did not work on this data with many silences and noises between words.

The remainder of this paper is organized as follows: in Section 2 we review related work, followed by a description of our data in Section 3. Section 4 provides a brief description of our speech recognizer as well as the experimental setup. Section 5 provides the results of our experiments, followed by a discussion in Section 6 and conclusions and future work in Section 7.

2 Related work

Following the seminal paper about the LISTEN project (Mostow et al. 1994), a number of studies have been conducted on using automatic speech recognition technology to score children's read speech.

Similar to automated assessment of adults' speech (Neumeyer, Franco et al. 2000; Witt, 1999), the likelihood computed in the Hidden Markov Model (HMM) decoding and some measurements of fluency, e.g., speaking rate, are widely used as features for predicting children's speaking proficiency. Children's speech is different than adults'. For example, children's speech exhibits higher fundamental frequencies (F0) than adults on average. Also, children's more limited knowledge of vocabulary and grammar results in more errors when reading printed text. Therefore, to achieve high-quality recognition on children's speech, modifications have to be made on recognizers that otherwise work well for adults.

In the LISTEN project (Mostow et al., 1994), the basic technology is to use speech recognition to classify each word of text as correctly read or not. Such a classification task is hard in that the children's speaking deviations from the text may include arbitrary words and non-words. In a study, they modeled variations by the modification of the lexicon and the language model of the Sphinx[1] speech recognizer.

Recently, the Technology Based Assessment of Language and Literacy project (TBALL, (Alwan, 2007)) has been attempting to assess and evaluate the language and literacy skills of young children automatically. In the TBALL project, a variety of tests including word verification, syllable blending, letter naming, and reading comprehension, are jointly used. Word verification is an assessment that measures the child's pronunciation of read-aloud target words. A traditional pronunciation verification method based on log-likelihoods from HMM models is used initially (Tepperman et al., 2006). Then an improvement based on a Bayesian network classifier (Tepperman et al., 2007) is em-

[1] See http://cmusphinx.sourceforge.net/html/cmusphinx.php

ployed to handle complicated errors such as pronunciation variations and other reading mistakes.

Many other approaches have been developed to further improve recognition performance on children's speech. For example, one highly accurate recognizer of children's speech has been developed by Hagen et al. (2007). Vocal tract length normalization (VTLN) has been utilized to cope with the children's different acoustic properties. Some special processing techniques, e.g., using a general garbage model to model all miscues in speaking, have been devised to improve the language model used in the recognition of children's speech (Li et al., 2007).

3 Data

For both system training and evaluation, we use a data set containing 3 passages read by the same 265 speakers (Set1) and a fourth passage (a longer version of Passage 1), read by a different set of 55 speakers (Set2). Further, we have word lists read by about 500 different speakers (Set3). All speakers from Set1[2] and most (84%) from the third set were U. S. middle school students in grades 6-8 (age 10-14). A smaller number of older students in grades 10-12 (age 15-18) was also included in the third set (16%).[3] [4]
In terms of native language, about 15% of Set1 and about 76% of Set3[5] are non-native speakers of English or list a language different from English as their preferred language.
Table 1 provides the details of these data sets. In the word lists data set, there are 178 different word lists containing 212 different word types in total (some word lists were read by several different students).

All data was manually transcribed using a spreadsheet where each word is presented in one line and the annotator, who listens to the audio file, has to mark-up any insertions, substitutions or deletions by the student.

Name	Recordings	Length in words
Passage 1 ("Bed", Set1-A)	265	158
Passage 2 ("Girls", Set1-B)	265	74
Passage 3 ("Keen", Set1-C)	265	100
Passage 4 ("Bed*") (Set2)	55	197
Word lists (Set3)	590	62 (average)

Table 1. Text passages and word lists data sets.

For ASR system training only, we additionally used parts of the OGI (Oregon Graduate Institute) and CMU (Carnegie Mellon University) Kids data sets as well (CSLU, 2008; LDC, 1997).

4 ASR system and experiments

The ASR system's acoustic model (AM) was trained using portions of the OGI and CMU Kids' corpora as well as a randomly selected sub-set of our own passage and word list data sets described in the previous section. About 90% of each data set (Set1, Set2, Set3) was used for that purpose. Since the size of our own data set was too small for AM training, we had to augment it with the two mentioned corpora (OGI, CMU Kids), although they were not a perfect match in age range and accent.
All recordings were first converted and down-sampled to 11 kHz, mono, 16 bit resolution, PCM format. There was no speaker overlap between training and test sets.

For the language model (LM), two different models were created: for passages, we built an interpolated trigram LM where 90% of the weight is assigned to a LM trained only on the 4 passages from the training set (Set1, Set2) and 10% to a generic LM using the Linguistic Data Consortium (LDC) Broadcast News corpus (LDC, 1997). The dictionary contains all words from the transcribed passages in the training set, augmented with the 1,000 most frequent words from the Broadcast News corpus. That way, the LM is not too restrictive and allows the recognizer to hypothesize some

[2] For Set1, we have demographics for 254 of 265 speakers (both for grade level and native language).
[3] Grade demographics are available for 477 speakers of Set3.
[4] We do not have demographic data for the small Set2 (55 speakers).
[5] This set (Set 3) has information on native language for 165 speakers.

reading mistakes not already encountered in the human transcriptions of the training set.

For the word lists, a trigram LM was found to be not working well since the words were spoken in isolation with sometimes significant pauses in between and automatic removal of these silences proved too hard given other confounding factors such as microphone, speaker, or background noise. Therefore it was decided to implement a grammar LM for the word list decoder where all possible words are present in a network that allows them to occur at any time and in any sequence, allowing for silence and/or noises in between words. This model with uniform priors, however, has the disadvantage of not including any words not present in the word list training set, such as common mispronunciations and is therefore more restrictive than the LM for text passages.

One could make the argument of using forced alignment instead of a statistical LM to determine reading errors. In fact, this approach is typically used when assessing the pronunciation of read speech. However, in our case, the interest is more in determining how many words were read correctly in the sequence of the text (and how fast they were read) as opposed to details in pronunciation. Further, even if we had confidence scores attached to words in forced alignment, deciding on which of the words obtained low confidence due to poor pronunciation or due to substitution would not be an easy decision. Finally, word deletions and insertions, if too frequent, might prevent the forced alignment algorithm from terminating.

After training was complete, we tested the recognizer on the held-out passage and word list data. After recognizing, we computed our target measure of "correct words per minute" (cwpm) according to the following formula (W= all words in a text, S= substitutions, D= deletions, T= reading time in minutes), performing a string alignment between the recognizer hypothesis and the passage or word list to be read:

$$(1) \qquad cwpm = \frac{W - S - D}{T}$$

The reason that insertions are not considered here is that they contribute to an increase in reading time and therefore can be considered to be accounted for already in the formula.

Next, we performed an experiment that looks at whether automatic scoring of read-aloud speech allows for accurate predictions of student placements in broad cohorts of reading proficiency.

We then also look more closely at typical errors made by human readers and the speech recognizer. All these experiments are described and discussed in the following section.

Table 2 describes the set-up of the experiments. Note that Passage4 (Set2) was included only in the training but not in the evaluation set since this set was very small. As mentioned in the previous section, most speakers from the passage sets read more than one passage and a few speakers from the word lists set read more than one word list.

Data set	Recordings	Speakers	Language model type
Passages1-3	101	37	Trigram
Word lists	42	38	Grammar

Table 2. Experiment set-up (evaluation sets).

5 Results

5.1 Overall results

Table 3 depicts the results of our evaluation run with the ASR system described above. Word accuracy is measured against the transcribed speaker reference (not against the true text that was read). Word accuracy is computed according to Equation (2), giving equal weight to reference and ASR hypothesis (c=correct, s=substitutions, d=deletions, i=insertions). This way, the formula is unbiased with respect to insertions or deletions:

$$(2) \qquad wacc = 0.5 \times 100.0 \times \left(\frac{c}{c+s+d} + \frac{c}{c+s+i} \right)$$

Data set	Recordings	Speakers	Average word Accuracy over all speech sample	Minimum word accuracy on a speech sample	Maximum word accuracy on a speech sample
All Passages (1-3)	101	37	72.2	20.4	93.8
Passage1 ("Bed")	28	28	70.8	20.4	83.6
Passage2 ("Girls")	36	36	64.1	25.4	85.7
Passage3 ("Keen")	37	37	77.7	27.4	93.8
Word lists	42	38	49.6	10.8	78.9

Table 3. ASR experiment results (word accuracies in percent)

The typical run-time on a 3.2GHz Pentium processor was less than 30 seconds for a recording (faster than real time).

We next compute cwpm measures for both human annotations (transcripts, "gold standard") and machine (ASR) hypotheses

Human annotators went over each read passage and word list and marked all reading errors of the speakers (here, only deletions and substitutions are relevant). The reading time is computed directly from the speech sample, so machine and human cwpm scores only differ in error counts of deletions and substitutions. Currently we only have one human annotation available per speech sample, but we aim to obtain a second annotation for the purpose of determining inter-annotator agreement.

Table 4 presents the overall results of comparing machine and human cwpm scoring. We performed both Pearson correlation as well as Spearman rank correlation. While the former provides a more generic measure of cwpm correlation, the latter focuses more on the question of the relative performance of different speakers compared to their peers which is usually the more interesting question in practical applications of reading assessment. Note that unlike for Table 3, the ASR hypotheses are now aligned with the text to be read since in a real-world application, no human transcriptions would be available.

We can see that despite the less than perfect recognition rate of the ASR system which causes a much lower average estimate for cwpm or cw (for word-lists), both Pearson and Spearman correlation coefficients are quite high, all above 0.7 for Spearman rank correlation and equal to 0.8 or higher for the Pearson product moment correlation. This is encouraging as it indicates that while current ASR technology is not yet able to exactly transcribe children's read speech, it is

Data set	Gold cwpm	ASR-based cwpm	Pearson r correlation	Spearman rank correlation
All Passages (1-3)	152.0	109.8	0.86	NA
Passage1 (Bed)	174.3	123.5	0.87	0.72
Passage2 (Girls)	133.1	86.5	0.86	0.73
Passage3 (Keen)	153.4	122.2	0.86	0.77
Word lists*	48.0	29.4	0.80	0.81

Table 4. CWPM results for passages and word lists. All correlations are significant at $p<0.01$.
*For word lists, we use "cw" (correct words, numerator of Equation (1)) as the measure, since students were not told to be rewarded for faster reading time here.

possible to use its output to compute reasonable read-aloud performance measures such as cwpm which can help to quickly and automatically assess reading proficiencies of students.

5.2 Cohort assignment experiment

To follow up on the encouraging results with basic and rank correlation, we conducted an experiment to explore the question of practical importance whether the automatic system can assign students to reading proficiency cohorts automatically.

For better comparison, we selected those 27 students from 37 total who read all 3 passages (Set 1) and grouped them into three cohorts of 9 students each, based on their human generated cwpm score for all passages combined: (a) proficient (cwpm>190), (b) intermediate (135<cwpm<190), and (c) low proficient (cwpm<135).

We then had the automatic system predict each student's cohort based on the cwpm computed from ASR. Since ASR-based cwpm values are consistently lower than human annotator based cwpm values, the automatic cohort assignment is not based on the cwpm values but rather on their ranking.

The outcome of this experiment is very encouraging in that there were no cohort prediction errors by the automatic system. While the precise ranking differs, the system is very well able to predict overall cohort placement of students based on cwpm.

5.3 Overall comparison of students' reading errors and ASR recognition errors

To look into more detail of what types of reading errors children make and to what extent they are reflected by the ASR system output, we used the sclite-tool by the National Institute for Standards and Technology (NIST, 2008) and performed two alignments on the evaluation set:

1. TRANS-TRUE: Alignment between human transcription and true passage or word list text to be read: this alignment informs us about the kinds of reading errors made by the students.
2. HYPO-TRANS: Alignment between the ASR hypotheses and the human transcriptions; this alignment informs us of ASR errors. (Note that this is different from the experiments reported in Table 4 above where we aligned the ASR hypotheses with the true reference texts to compute cwpm.)

Table 5 provides general statistics on these two alignments.

Data set	Alignment	SUB	DEL	INS
Passages 1-3	TRANS-TRUE	2.0%	6.1%	1.8%
Pas-sages1-3	HYPO-TRANS	18.7%	9.6%	8.1%
Word lists	TRANS-TRUE	5.6%	6.2%	0.6%
Word lists	HYPO-TRANS	42.0%	8.9%	6.4%

Table 5. Word error statistics on TRANS-TRUE and HYPO-TRANS alignments for both evaluation data sets.

From Table 5 we can see that while for students, deletions occur more frequently than substitutions and, in particular, insertions, the ASR system, due to its imperfect recognition, generates mostly substitutions, in particular for the word lists where the word accuracy is only around 50%.

Further, we observe that the students' average reading word error rate (only taking into account substitutions and deletions as we did above for the cwpm and cw measures) lies around 8% for passages and 12% for wordlists (all measured on the held-out evaluation data).

5.4 Specific examples

Next, we look at some examples of frequent confusion pairs for those 4 combinations of data sets and alignments. Table 6 lists the top 5 most frequent confusion pairs (i.e., substitutions).

For passages, all of the most frequent reading errors by students are morphological variants of the target words, whereas this is only true for some of the ASR errors, while other ASR errors can be far off the target words. For word lists, student errors are sometimes just orthographically related to the target word (e.g., "liner" instead of "linear"), and sometimes of different part-of-speech (e.g., "equally" instead of "equality"). ASR errors are typically related to the target word by some phonetic similarity (e.g., "example" instead of "simple").

Finally, we look at a comparison between errors made by the students and the fraction of those correctly identified by the ASR system in the recognition hypotheses. Table 7 provides the statistics on these matched errors for text passages and word lists.

Data set	Alignment	Reference	Spoken/ recognized	Count
Passages 1-3	TRANS-TRUE	asks	ask	6
		savings	saving	5
		projects	project	4
		teacher's	teacher	4
		time	times	4
Passages 1-3	HYPO-TRANS	storm	storms	11
		lee's	be	6
		lee's	we	6
		observer	and	6
		thousand	the	6
Word lists	TRANS-TRUE	nature	Natural	6
		oversleep	overslept	5
		equality	equally	4
		linear	liner	4
		warehoused	warehouse	3
Word lists	HYPO-TRANS	plan	planned	8
		see	season	6
		simple	example	6
		unofficial	competition	5
		loud	throughout	4

Table 6. Top 5 most frequent confusion pairs for passages and word list evaluation sets in two different alignments. For passages, substitutions among closed class words such as determiners or prepositions are omitted.

Table 7 shows that while for text passages, almost half of the relevant errors (substitutions and deletions) were correctly identified by the recognizer, for word lists, this percentage is substantially smaller.

6 Discussion

The goal of this paper is to evaluate the possibility of creating a system for automatic oral reading assessment for middle school children, based on text passages and word lists.
We decided to use the common reading proficiency measure of "correct words per minute" which enables us to align ASR word hypotheses with the correct texts, estimate cwpm based on this alignment and the reading time, and then compare the automatically estimated cwpm with human annotations of the same texts.

Data set / error type	Percentage of correctly identified errors
Passages 1-3 – SUB	20.6
Passages 1-3 – DEL	56.4
Passages 1-3 – SUB+DEL	47.7
Word lists – SUB	2.7
Word lists – DEL	29.4
Word lists – SUB+DEL	16.8

Table 7. Statistics on matched errors: percentage of students' reading errors (substitutions and deletions) that were also correctly identified by the ASR system.

We built a recognizer with an acoustic model based on CMU and OGI kids' corpora as well as about 90% of our own text passages and word list data (Sets 1-3). For the in-context reading (text passages) we trained a trigram model focused mostly on transcriptions of the passages. For the out-of-context isolated word reading, we used a grammar language model where every possible word of the word lists in the training set can follow any other word at any time, with silence and/or noise between words. (While this was not our preferred choice, standard n-gram language models performed very poorly given the difficulty of removing inter-word silences or noise automatically.)
Given how hard ASR for children's speech is and given our small matched data sets, the word accuracy of 72% for text passages was not unreasonable and was acceptable, particularly in a first development cycle. The word accuracy of only about 50% for word lists, however, is more prob-

lematic and we conjecture that the two main reasons for the worse performance were (a) the absence of time stamps for the location of words which made it sometimes hard for the recognizer to locate the correct segment in the signal for word decoding (given noises in between), and (b) the sometimes poor recording conditions where volumes were set too high or too low, too much background or speaker noise was present etc. Further, the high relative number of non-native speakers in that data set may also have contributed to the lower word accuracy of the word lists.

While the current data collection had not been done with speech recognition in mind, in future data collection efforts, we will make sure that the sound quality of recordings is better monitored, with some initial calibration, and that we store time stamps when words are presented on the screen to facilitate the recognition task and to allow the recognizer to expect one particular word at one particular point in time.

Despite imperfect word accuracies, however, for both passages and word lists we found encouragingly high correlations between human and automatic cwpm measures (cw measures for word lists). Obviously, the absolute values of cwpm differ greatly as the ASR system generates many more errors on average than the readers, but both Pearson correlation as well as Spearman rank correlation measures are all above 0.7. This means that if we would use our automatic scoring results to rank students' reading proficiency, the ranking order would be overall quite similar to an order produced by human annotators. This observation about the rank, rather than the absolute value of cwpm, is important in so far as it is often the case that educators are interested in separating "cohorts" of readers with similar proficiency and in particular to identify the lowest performing cohort for additional reading practice and tutoring.

An experiment testing the ability of the system to place students into three reading proficiency cohorts based on cwpm was very encouraging in that all 27 students of the test set were placed in the correct cohort by the system.

When we compare frequent student errors with those made by the machine (Table 6), we see that often times, students just substitute slight morphological variants (e.g., "ask" for "asks"), whereas in the ASR system, errors are typically more complex than just simple substitutions of morphological variants. However, in the case of word lists, we do find substitutions with related phonological content in the ASR output (e.g., "example" for "simple").

Finally, we observed that, only for the text passages, the ASR system could correctly identify a substantial percentage of readers' substitutions and deletions (about 48%, see Table 7). This is also encouraging as it is a first step towards meaningful feedback in a potential interactive setting. However, we here only look at recall – because of the much larger number of ASR substitutions, precision is much lower and therefore the risk of overcorrection (false alarms) is still quite high.

Despite all of the current shortcomings, we feel that we were able to demonstrate a "proof-of-concept" with our initial system in that we can use our trained ASR system to make reliable estimates on students' reading proficiency as measured with "correct words per minute", where correlations between human and machine scores are in the 0.80-0.86 range for text passages and word lists.

7 Conclusions and future work

This paper demonstrates the feasibility of building an automatic scoring system for middle school students' reading proficiency, using a targeted trained speech recognition system and the widely used measure of "correctly read words per minute" (cwpm).

The speech recognizer was trained both on external data (OGI and CMU kids' corpora) and internal data (text passages and word lists), yielding two different modes for text passages (trigram language model) and word lists (grammar language model).

Automatically estimated cwpm measures agreed closely with human cwpm measures, achieving 0.8 and higher correlation with Pearson and 0.7 and higher correlation with Spearman rank correlation measures.

Future work includes an improved set-up for recordings such as initial calibration and on-line sound quality monitoring, adding time stamps to recordings of word lists, adding more data for training/adaptation of the ASR system, and exploring other features (such as fluency features) and their potential role in cwpm prediction.

Acknowledgements

The authors would like to acknowledge the contributions of Kathy Sheehan, Tenaha O'Reilly and Kelly Bruce to this work. We further are grateful for the useful feedback and suggestions from our colleagues at ETS and the anonymous reviewers that greatly helped improve our paper.

References

Alwan, A. (2007). A System for Technology Based Assessment of Language and Literacy in Young Children: the Role of Multiple Information Sources. Proceedings of MMSP, Greece.

Center for Spoken Language Understanding (CSLU), 2008. Kids' Speech Corpus, http://www.cslu.ogi.edu/corpora/kids/.LDC, BN.

Deno, S. L., Fuchs, L. S., Marston, D., & Shin, J. (2001). Using curriculum-based measurements to establish growth standards for students with learning disabilities. School Psychology Review, 30(4), 507-524.

Deno, S. L. and D. Marsten (2006). Curriculum-based measurement of oral reading: An indicator of growth in fluency. What Research Has to Say about Fluency Instruction. S. J. Samuels and A. E. Farstrup. Newark, DE, International Reading Association: 179-203.

Hagen, A., B. Pellom, & R. Cole. (2007). "Highly accurate children's speech recognition for interactive reading tutors using subword units." Speech Communication **49**(6): 861-873.

Lee, S., A. Potamianos, & S. Narayanan. (1999). "Acoustics of children's speech: developmental changes of temporal and spectral parameters." Journal of Acoustics Society of American (JASA) 105: 1455-1468.

Li, X., Y. C. Ju, L. Deng & A. Acero. (2007). Efficient and Robust Language Modeling in an Automatic Children's Reading Tutor System. Proc. IEEE International Conference on Acoustics, Speech and Signal Processing ICASSP 2007.

Li, Q. and M. Russell (2002). An analysis of the causes of increased error rates in children's speech recognition. ICSLP. Denver, CO.

Linguistic Data Consortium (LDC), 1997. 1996 English Broadcast News Speech (HUB4), LDC97S44.

Linguistic Data Consortium (LDC), 1997. The CMU Kids Corpus, LDC97S63.

Mostow, J., S. F. Roth, G. Hauptmann & M. Kane. (1994). A prototype reading coach that listens. AAAI '94: Proceedings of the twelfth national conference on Artificial intelligence, Menlo Park, CA, USA, American Association for Artificial Intelligence.

National Center of Educational Statistics. (2006). National Assessment of Educational Progress. Washington DC: U.S. Government Printing Office.

National Institute for Standards and Technology (NIST), 2008. Sclite software package. http://www.nist.gov/speech/tools/

Neumeyer, L., H. Franco, V. Digalakis & M. Weintraub. (2000). "Automatic Scoring of Pronunciation Quality." Speech Communication **6**.

No Child Left Behind Act of 2001, Pub. L. No. 107-110, 115 Stat. 1425 (2002).

Tepperman, J., J. Silva, A. Kazemzadeh, H. You, S. Lee, A. Alwan & S. Narayanan. (2006). Pronunciation verification of children's speech for automatic literacy assessment. INTERSPEECH-2006. Pittsburg, PA.

Tepperman, J., M. Black, P. Price, S. Lee, A. Kazemzadeh, M. Gerosa, M. Heritage, A. Alwan & S. Narayanan.(2007). A bayesian network classifier for word-level reading assessment. Proceedings of ICSLP, Antwerp, Belgium.

Wayman, M. M., Wallace, T., Wiley, H. I., Ticha, R., & Espin, C. A. (2007). Literature synthesis on curriculum-based measurement in reading. The Journal of Special Education, 41(2), 85-120.

Witt, S. M. (1999). Use of Speech Recognition in Computer-assisted Language Learning, University of Cambridge.

Inferring Tutorial Dialogue Structure with Hidden Markov Modeling

Kristy Elizabeth Boyer[a] | Eun Young Ha[a] | Robert Phillips[ab] | Michael D. Wallis[ab] | Mladen A. Vouk[a] | James C. Lester[a]

[a]Department of Computer Science, North Carolina State University
[b]Applied Research Associates
Raleigh, NC, USA

{keboyer, eha, rphilli, mdwallis, vouk, lester}@ncsu.edu

Abstract

The field of intelligent tutoring systems has seen many successes in recent years. A significant remaining challenge is the automatic creation of corpus-based tutorial dialogue management models. This paper reports on early work toward this goal. We identify tutorial dialogue *modes* in an unsupervised fashion using hidden Markov models (HMMs) trained on input sequences of manually-labeled dialogue acts and adjacency pairs. The two best-fit HMMs are presented and compared with respect to the dialogue structure they suggest; we also discuss potential uses of the methodology for future work.

1 Introduction

The field of intelligent tutoring systems has made great strides toward bringing the benefits of one-on-one tutoring to a wider population of learners. Some intelligent tutoring systems, called *tutorial dialogue systems*, support learners by engaging in rich natural language dialogue, *e.g.*, (Graesser *et al.* 2003; Zinn, Moore & Core 2002; Evens & Michael 2006; Aleven, Koedinger & Popescu 2003; Litman *et al.* 2006; Arnott, Hastings & Allbritton 2008; VanLehn *et al.* 2002). However, creating these systems comes at a high cost: it entails handcrafting each pedagogical strategy the tutor might use and then realizing these strategies in a dialogue management framework that is also custom-engineered for the application. It is hoped that the next generation of these systems can leverage corpora of tutorial dialogue in order to provide more robust dialogue management models that capture the discourse phenomena present in effective natural language tutoring.

The structure of tutorial dialogue has traditionally been studied by manually examining corpora and focusing on cognitive and motivational aspects of tutorial strategies (*e.g.*, Lepper *et al.* 1993; Graesser, Person & Magliano 1995). While these approaches yielded foundational results for the field, such analyses suffer from two serious limitations: manual approaches are not easily scalable to different or larger corpora, and the rigidity of handcrafted dialogue structure tagging schemes may not capture all the phenomena that occur in practice.

In contrast, the stochastic nature of dialogue lends itself to description through probabilistic models. In tutorial dialogue, some early work has adapted language processing techniques, namely *n*-gram analyses, to examine human tutors' responses to student uncertainty (Forbes-Riley & Litman 2005), as well as to find correlations between local tutoring strategies and student outcomes (Boyer *et al.* 2008). However, this work is limited by its consideration of small dialogue windows.

Looking at a broader window of turns is often accomplished by modeling the dialogue as a Markov decision process. With this approach,

Proceedings of the NAACL HLT Workshop on Innovative Use of NLP for Building Educational Applications, pages 19–26,
Boulder, Colorado, June 2009.

techniques such as reinforcement learning can be used to compare potential policies in terms of effectiveness for student learning. Determining relevant feature sets (Tetreault & Litman 2008) and conducting focussed experiments for localized strategy effectiveness (Chi *et al.* 2008) are active areas of research in this line of investigation. These approches often fix the dialogue structures under consideration in order to compare the outcomes associated with those structures or the features that influence policy choice.

In contrast to treating dialogue structure as a fixed entity, one approach for modeling the progression of complete dialogues involves learning the higher-level structure in order to infer succinct probabilistic models of the interaction. For example, data-driven approaches for discovering dialogue structure have been applied to corpora of human-human task-oriented dialogue using general models of task structure (Bangalore, Di Fabbrizio & Stent 2006). Encouraging results have emerged from using a general model of the task structure to inform automatic dialogue act tagging as well as subtask segmentation.

Our current work examines a modeling technique that does not require *a priori* knowledge of the task structure: specifically, we propose to use hidden Markov models (HMMs) (Rabiner 1989) to capture the structure of tutorial dialogue implicit within sequences of tagged dialogue acts. Such probablistic inference of discourse structure has been used in recent work with HMMs for topic identification (Barzilay & Lee 2004) and related graphical models for segmenting multi-party spoken discourse (Purver *et al.* 2006). Analogously, our current work focuses on identifying dialogic structures that emerge during tutorial dialogue. Our approach is based on the premise that at any given point in the tutorial dialogue, the collaborative interaction is "in" a dialogue *mode* (Cade *et al.* 2008) that characterizes the nature of the exchanges between tutor and student; these modes correspond to the hidden states in the HMM. Results to date suggest that meaningful descriptive models of tutorial dialogue can be generated by this simple stochastic modeling technique. This paper focuses on the comparison of two first-order HMMs: one trained on sequences of dialogue acts, and the second trained on sequences of adjacency pairs.

2 Corpus Analysis

The HMMs were trained on a corpus of human-human tutorial dialogue collected in the domain of introductory computer science. Forty-three learners interacted remotely with one of fourteen tutors through a keyboard-to-keyboard remote learning environment yielding 4,864 dialogue moves.

2.1 Dialogue Act Tagging

The tutoring corpus was manually tagged with dialogue acts designed to capture the salient characteristics of the tutoring process (Table 1).

Tag	Act	Example
Q	Question	*Where should I Declare i?*
EQ	Evaluation Question	*How does that look?*
S	Statement	*You need a closing brace.*
G	Grounding	*Ok.*
EX	Extra-Domain	*You may use your book.*
PF	Positive Feedback	*Yes, that's right.*
LF	Lukewarm Feedback	*Sort of.*
NF	Negative Feedback	*No, that's not right.*

Table 1. Dialogue Act Tags

The correspondence between utterances and dialogue act tags is one-to-one; compound utterances were split by the primary annotator prior to the inter-rater reliability study.[1] This dialogue act tagging effort produced sequences of dialogue acts that have been used in their un-altered forms to train one of the two HMMs presented here (Section 3).

2.2 Adjacency Pair Identification

In addition to the HMM trained on sequences of individual dialogue acts, another HMM was trained on sequences of dialogue act adjacency pairs. The importance of adjacency pairs is well-established in natural language dialogue (*e.g.*, Schlegoff & Sacks 1973), and adjacency pair analysis has illuminated important phenomena in tutoring as well (Forbes-Riley *et al.* 2007). The

[1] Details of the study procedure used to collect the corpus, as well as Kappa statistics for inter-rater reliability, are reported in (Boyer *et al.* 2008).

intuition behind adjacency pairs is that certain dialogue acts naturally occur together, and by grouping these acts we capture an exchange between two conversants in a single structure. This formulation is of interest for our purposes because when treating sequences of dialogue acts as a Markov process, with or without hidden states, the addition of adjacency pairs may offer a semantically richer observation alphabet.

To find adjacency pairs we utilize a χ^2 test for independence of the categorical variables act_i and act_{i+1} for all sequential pairs of dialogue acts that occur in the corpus. Only pairs in which speaker(act_i) $\neq$ speaker(act_{i+1}) were considered. Table 2 displays a list of all dependent adjacency pairs sorted by descending (unadjusted) statistical significance; the subscript on each dialogue act tag indicates tutor (*t*) or student (*s*).

An adjacency pair joining algorithm was applied to join statistically significant pairs of dialogue acts (p<0.01) into atomic units according to a priority determined by the strength of the statistical significance. Dialogue acts that were "left out" of adjacency pair groupings were treated as atomic elements in subsequent analysis. Figure 1 illustrates the application of the adjacency pair joining algorithm on a sequence of dialogue acts from the corpus.

Original dialogue act sequence:

$G_s \rightarrow G_t \rightarrow Q_s \rightarrow S_t \rightarrow EQ_t \rightarrow EQ_s \rightarrow PF_t \rightarrow Q_s$

After adjacency pair joining:

$G_sG_t \rightarrow Q_sS_t \rightarrow EQ_t \rightarrow EQ_sPF_t \rightarrow Q_sS_t$

Figure 1. DA Sequence Before/After Joining

3 HMM of Dialogue Structure

A hidden Markov model is defined by three constituents: 1) the set of *hidden states* (dialogue modes), each characterized by its emission probability distribution over the possible *observations* (dialogue acts and/or adjacency pairs), 2) the transition probability matrix among *observations* (dialogue acts and/or adjacency pairs), 2) the transition probability matrix among

act_i	act_{i+1}	P(act_{i+1}| act_i)	P(act_{i+1}| $\neg act_i$)	χ^2 val	*p*-val
EQ_s	PF_t	0.48	0.07	654	<0.0001
G_s	G_t	0.27	0.03	380	<0.0001
EX_s	EX_t	0.34	0.03	378	<0.0001
EQ_t	PF_s	0.18	0.01	322	<0.0001
EQ_t	S_s	0.24	0.03	289	<0.0001
EQ_s	LF_t	0.13	0.01	265	<0.0001
Q_t	S_s	0.65	0.04	235	<0.0001
EQ_t	LF_s	0.07	0.00	219	<0.0001
Q_s	S_t	0.82	0.38	210	<0.0001
EQ_s	NF_t	0.08	0.01	207	<0.0001
EX_t	EX_s	0.19	0.02	177	<0.0001
NF_s	G_t	0.29	0.03	172	<0.0001
EQ_t	NF_s	0.11	0.01	133	<0.0001
S_s	G_t	0.16	0.03	95	<0.0001
S_s	PF_t	0.30	0.10	90	<0.0001
S_t	G_s	0.07	0.04	36	<0.0001
PF_s	G_t	0.14	0.04	34	<0.0001
LF_s	G_t	0.22	0.04	30	<0.0001
S_t	EQ_s	0.11	0.07	29	<0.0001
G_t	EX_s	0.07	0.03	14	0.002
S_t	Q_s	0.07	0.05	14	0.0002
G_t	G_s	0.10	0.05	9	0.0027
EQ_t	EQ_s	0.13	0.08	8	0.0042

Table 2. All Dependent Adjacency Pairs

hidden states, and 3) the initial hidden state (dialogue mode) probability distribution.

3.1 Discovering Number of Dialogue Modes

In keeping with the goal of automatically discovering dialogue structure, it was desirable to learn *n,* the best number of hidden states for the HMM, during modeling. To this end, we trained and ten-fold cross-validated seven models, each featuring randomly-initialized parameters, for each number of hidden states *n* from 2 to 15, inclusive.[2] The average log-likelihood fit from ten-fold cross-

[2] n=15 was chosen as an initial maximum number of states because it comfortably exceeded our hypothesized range of 3 to 7 (informed by the tutoring literature). The Akaike Information Criterion measure steadily worsened above n = 5, confirming no need to train models with n > 15.

validation was computed across all seven models for each n, and this average log-likelihood l_n was used to compute the Akaike Information Criterion, a maximum-penalized likelihood estimator that prefers simpler models (Scott 2002). This modeling approach was used to train HMMs on both the dialogue act and the adjacency pair input sequences.

3.2 Best-Fit Models

The input sequences of individual dialogue acts contain 16 unique symbols because each of the 8 dialogue act tags (Table 1) was augmented with a label of the speaker, either tutor or student. The best-fit HMM for this input sequence contains n_{DA}=5 hidden states. The adjacency pair input sequences contain 39 unique symbols, including all dependent adjacency pairs (Table 2) along with all individual dialogue acts because each dialogue act occurs at some point outside an adjacency pair. The best-fit HMM for this input sequence contains n_{AP}=4 hidden states. In both cases, the best-fit number of dialogue modes implied by the hidden states is within the range of what is often considered in traditional tutorial dialogue analysis (Cade *et al.* 2008; Graesser, Person & Magliano 1995).

4 Analysis

Evaluating the impact of grouping the dialogue acts into adjacency pairs requires a fine-grained examination of the generated HMMs to gain insight into how each model interprets the student sessions.

4.1 Dialogue Act HMM

Figure 2 displays the emission probability distributions for the dialogue act HMM. State 0_{DA}, *Tutor Lecture*,[3] is strongly dominated by tutor statements with some student questions and positive tutor feedback. State 1_{DA} constitutes *Grounding/Extra-Domain*, a conversational state consisting of acknowledgments, backchannels, and discussions that do not relate to the computer science task. State 2_{DA}, *Student Reflection*, generates student evaluation questions, statements, and positive and negative feedback. State 3_{DA} is comprised of tutor utterances, with positive feedback occurring most commonly followed by statements, grounding, lukewarm feedback, and negative feedback. This state is interpreted as a *Tutor Feedback* mode. Finally, State 4_{DA}, *Tutor Lecture/Probing*, is characterized by tutor statements and evaluative questions with some student grounding statements.

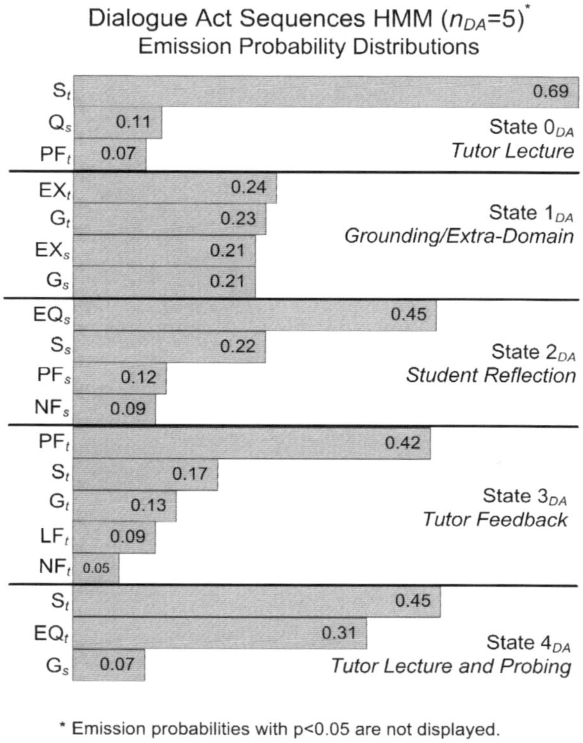

Figure 2. Emission Probability Distributions for Dialogue Act HMM

The state transition diagram (Figure 3) illustrates that *Tutor Lecture* (0_{DA}) and *Grounding/Extra-Domain* (1_{DA}) are stable states whose probability of self-transition is high: 0.75 and 0.79, respectively. Perhaps not surprisingly, *Student Reflection* (2_{DA}) is most likely to transition to *Tutor Feedback* (3_{DA}) with probability 0.77. *Tutor Feedback* (3_{DA}) transitions to *Tutor Lecture* (0_{DA}) with probability 0.60, *Tutor Lecture/Probing* (4_{DA}) with probability 0.26, and *Student Reflection* (2_{DA}) with probability 0.09. Finally, *Tutor Lecture/Probing* (4_{DA}) very often transitions to *Student Reflection* (2_{DA}) with probability 0.82.

[3] For simplicity, the states of each HMM have been named according to an intuitive interpretation of the emission probability distribution.

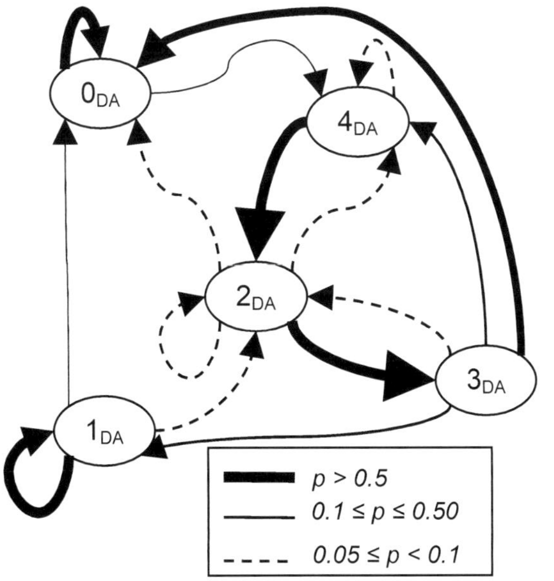

Figure 3. Transition diagram for dialogue act HMM

4.2 Adjacency Pair HMM

Figure 4 displays the emission probability distributions for the HMM that was trained on the input sequences of adjacency pairs. State 0_{AP}, *Tutor Lecture*, consists of tutorial statements, positive feedback, and dialogue turns initiated by student questions. In this state, student evaluation questions occur in adjacency pairs with positive tutor feedback, and other student questions are answered by tutorial statements. State 1_{AP}, *Tutor Evaluation*, generates primarily tutor evaluation questions, along with the adjacency pair of tutorial statements followed by student acknowledgements. State 2_{AP} generates conversational grounding and extra-domain talk; this *Grounding/Extra-Domain* state is dominated by the adjacency pair of student grounding followed by tutor grounding. State 3_{AP} is comprised of several adjacency pairs: student questions followed by tutor answers, student statements with positive tutor feedback, and student evaluation questions followed by positive feedback. This *Question/Answer* state also generates some tutor grounding and student evaluation questions outside of adjacency pairs.

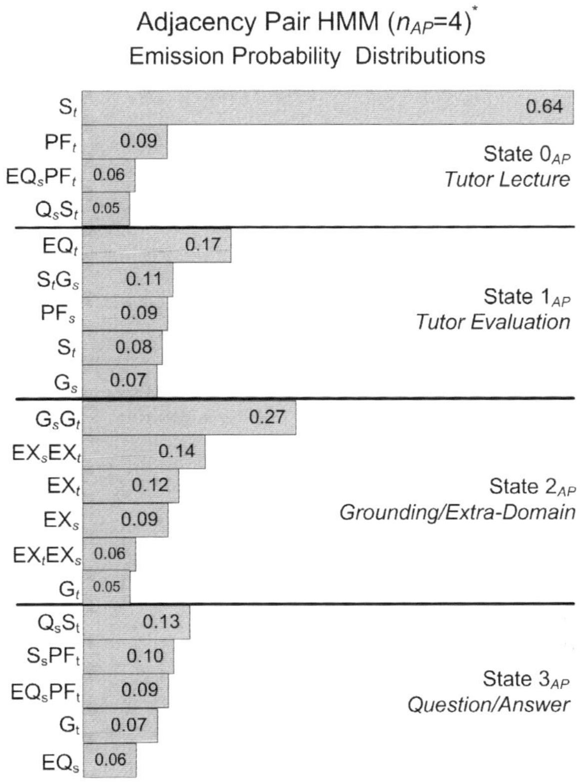

* Emission probabilities with p<0.05 are not displayed.

Figure 4. Emission Probability Distributions for Adjacency Pair HMM

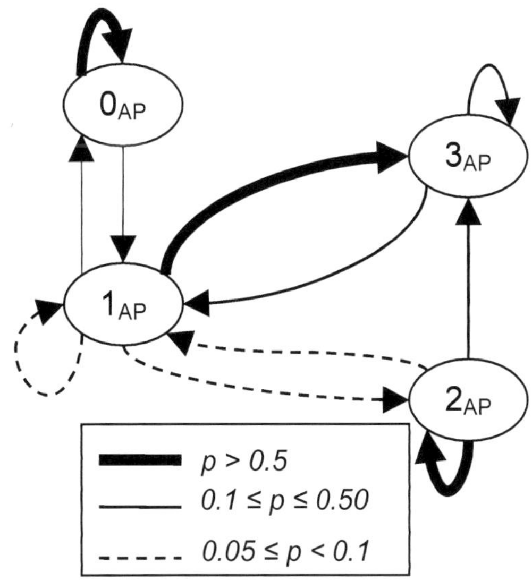

Figure 5. Transition diagram for adjacency pair HMM

4.3 Dialogue Mode Sequences

In order to illustrate how the above models fit the data, Figure 6 depicts the progression of dialogue modes that generate an excerpt from the corpus.

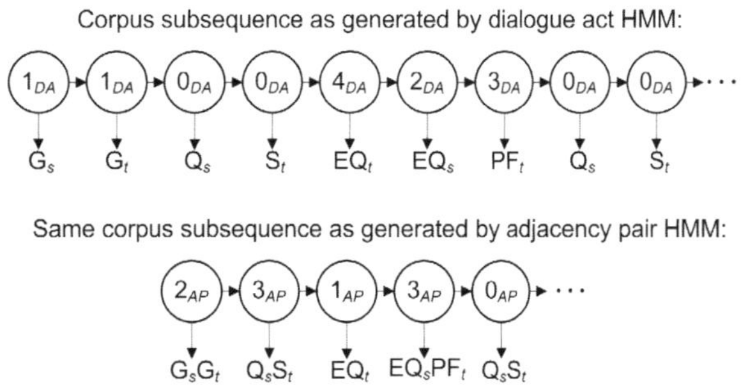

Figure 6. Best-fit sequences of hidden states

In both models, the most commonly-occurring dialogue mode is *Tutor Lecture*, which generates 45% of observations in the dialogue act model and around 60% in the adjacency pair model. Approximately 15% of the dialogue act HMM observations are fit to each of states *Student Reflection*, *Tutor Feedback*, and *Tutor Lecture/Probing*. This model spends the least time, around 8%, in *Grounding/Extra Domain.* The adjacency pair model fits approximately 15% of its observations to each of *Tutor Evaluation* and *Question/Answer*, with around 8% in *Grounding/Extra-Domain*.

4.4 Model Comparison

While the two models presented here describe the same corpus, it is important to exercise caution when making direct structural comparisons. The models contain neither the same number of hidden states nor the same emission symbol alphabet; therefore, our comparison will be primarily qualitative. It is meaningful to note, however, that the adjacency pair model with n_{AP}=4 achieved an average log-likelihood fit on the training data that was 5.8% better than the same measure achieved by the dialogue act model with n_{DA}=5, despite the adjacency pair input sequences containing greater than twice the number of unique symbols.[4]

[4] This comparison is meaningful because the models depicted here provided the best fit among all sizes of models trained for the same input scenario.

Our qualitative comparison begins by examining the modes that are highly similar in the two models. State 2_{AP} generates grounding and extra-domain statements, as does State 1_{DA}. These two states both constitute a *Grounding/Extra-Domain* dialogue mode. One artifact of the tutoring study design is that all sessions begin in this state due to a compulsory greeting that signaled the start of each session. More precisely, the initial state probability distribution for each HMM assigns probability 1 to this state and probability 0 to all other states.

Another dialogue mode that is structurally similar in the two models is *Tutor Lecture*, in which the majority of utterances are tutor statements. This mode is captured in State 0 in both models, with State 0_{AP} implying more detail than State 0_{DA} because it is certain in the former that some of the tutor statements and positive feedback occurred in response to student questions. While student questions are present in State 0_{DA}, no such precise ordering of the acts can be inferred, as discussed in Section 1.

Other states do not have one-to-one correspondence between the two models. State 2_{DA}, *Student Reflection,* generates only student utterances and the self-transition probability for the state is very low; the dialogue usually visits State 2_{DA} for one turn and then transitions immediately to another state. Although this aspect of the model reflects the fact that students rarely keep the floor for more than one utterance at a time in the corpus, such quick dialogue mode transitions are inconsistent with an intuitive understanding of tutorial dialogue modes as meta-structures that usually encompass more than one dialogue turn. This phenomenon is perhaps more accurately captured in the adjacency pair model. For example, the dominant dialogue act of State 2_{DA} is a student evaluation question (EQ_s). In contrast, these dialogue acts are generated as part of an adjacency pair by State 3_{AP}; this model joins the student questions with subsequent positive feedback from the tutor rather than generating the question and then transitioning to a new dialogue mode. Further addressing the issue of frequent state transitions is discussed as future work in Section 6.

5 Discussion and Limitations

Overall, the adjacency pair model is preferable for our purposes because its structure lends itself more readily to interpretation as a set of dialogue modes each of which encompasses more than one dialogue move. This structural property is guaranteed by the inclusion of adjacency pairs as atomic elements. In addition, although the set of emission symbols increased to include significant adjacency pairs along with all dialogue acts, the log-likelihood fit of this model was slightly higher than the same measure for the HMM trained on the sequences of dialogue acts alone. The remainder of this section focuses on properties of the adjacency pair model.

One promising result of this early work emerges from the fact that by applying hidden Markov modeling to sequences of adjacency pairs, meaningful dialogue modes have emerged that are empirically justified. The number of these dialogue modes is consistent with what researchers have traditionally used as a set of hypothesized tutorial dialogue modes. Moreover, the composition of the dialogue modes reflects some recognizable aspects of tutoring sessions: tutors teach through the *Tutor Lecture* mode and give feedback on student knowledge in a *Tutor Evaluation* mode. Students ask questions and state their own perception of their knowledge in a *Question/Answer* mode. Both parties engage in "housekeeping" talk containing such things as greetings and acknowledgements, and sometimes, even in a controlled environment, extra-domain conversation occurs between the conversants in the *Grounding/Extra-Domain* mode.

Although the tutorial modes discovered may not map perfectly to sets of handcrafted tutorial dialogue modes from the literature (*e.g.,* Cade *et al.* 2008), it is rare for such a perfect mapping to exist even between those sets of handcrafted modes. In addition, the HMM framework allows for succinct probabilistic description of the phenomena at work during the tutoring session: through the state transition matrix, we can see the back-and-forth flow of the dialogue among its modes.

6 Conclusions and Future Work

Automatically learning dialogue structure is an important step toward creating more robust tutorial dialogue management systems. We have presented two hidden Markov models in which the hidden states are interpreted as *dialogue modes* for task-oriented tutorial dialogue. These models were learned in an unsupervised fashion from manually-labeled dialogue acts. HMMs offer concise stochastic models of the complex interaction patterns occurring in natural language tutorial dialogue. The evidence suggests this methodology, which as presented requires only a sequence of dialogue acts as input, holds promise for automatically discovering the structure of tutorial dialogue.

Future work will involve conducting evaluations to determine the benefits gained by using HMMs compared to simpler statistical models. In addition, it is possible that more general types of graphical models will prove useful in overcoming some limitations of HMMs, such as their arbitrarily frequent state transitions, to more readily capture the phenomena of interest. The descriptive insight offered by these exploratory models may also be increased by future work in which the input sequences are enhanced with information about the surface-level content of the utterance. In addition, knowledge of the task state within the tutoring session can be used to segment the dialogue in meaningful ways to further refine model structure.

It is also hoped that these models can identify empirically-derived tutorial dialogue structures that can be associated with measures of effectiveness such as student learning (Soller & Stevens 2007). These lines of investigation could inform the development of next-generation natural language tutorial dialogue systems.

Acknowledgments

Thanks to Marilyn Walker and Dennis Bahler for insightful early discussions on the dialogue and machine learning aspects of this work, respectively. This research was supported by the National Science Foundation under Grants REC-0632450, IIS-0812291, CNS-0540523, and GRFP. Any opinions, findings, and conclusions or recommendations expressed in this material are those of the authors and do not necessarily reflect the views of the National Science Foundation.

References

Aleven, V., K. Koedinger, and O. Popescu. 2003. A tutorial dialog system to support self-explanation: Evaluation and open questions. *Proceedings of the 11th International Conference on Artificial Intelligence in Education*: 39-46.

Arnott, E., P. Hastings, and D. Allbritton. 2008. Research methods tutor: Evaluation of a dialogue-based tutoring system in the classroom. *Behavioral Research Methods* 40(3): 694-698.

Bangalore, S., Di Fabbrizio, G., and Stent, A. 2006. Learning the structure of task-driven human-human dialogs. *Proceedings of the 21st International Conference on Computational Linguistics and 44th Annual Meeting of the ACL*: 201-208.

Barzilay, R., and Lee, L. 2004. Catching the drift: Probabilistic content models, with applications to generation and summarization. *Proceedings of NAACL HLT*: 113–120.

Boyer, K. E., Phillips, R., Wallis, M., Vouk, M., and Lester, J. 2008. Balancing cognitive and motivational scaffolding in tutorial dialogue. *Proceedings of the 9th International Conference on Intelligent Tutoring Systems*: 239-249.

Cade, W., Copeland, J., Person, N., and D'Mello, S. 2008. Dialog modes in expert tutoring. *Proceedings of the 9th International Conference on Intelligent Tutoring Systems*: 470-479.

Chi, M., Jordan, P., VanLehn, K., and Hall, M. 2008. Reinforcement learning-based feature selection for developing pedagogically effective tutorial dialogue tactics. *Proceedings of the 1st International Conference on Educational Data Mining*: 258-265.

Evens, M., and J. Michael. 2006. *One-on-one tutoring by humans and computers*. Lawrence Erlbaum Associates, Mahwah, New Jersey.

Forbes-Riley, K., and Litman, D. J. 2005. Using bigrams to identify relationships between student certainness states and tutor responses in a spoken dialogue corpus. *Proceedings of the 6th SIGdial Workshop on Discourse and Dialogue*: 87-96.

Forbes-Riley, K., Rotaru, M., Litman, D. J., and Tetreault, J. 2007. Exploring affect-context dependencies for adaptive system development. *Proceedings of NAACL HLT*: 41-44.

Graesser, A., G. Jackson, E. Mathews, H. Mitchell, A. Olney, M. Ventura, and P. Chipman. 2003. Why/AutoTutor: A test of learning gains from a physics tutor with natural language dialog. *Proceedings of the Twenty-Fifth Annual Conference of the Cognitive Science Society*: 1-6.

Graesser, A. C., N. K. Person, and J. P. Magliano. 1995. Collaborative dialogue patterns in naturalistic one-to-one tutoring. *Applied Cognitive Psychology* 9(6): 495–522.

Lepper, M. R., M. Woolverton, D. L. Mumme, and J. L. Gurtner. 1993. Motivational techniques of expert human tutors: Lessons for the design of computer-based tutors. Pages 75-105 in S. P. Lajoie, and S. J. Derry, editors. *Computers as cognitive tools*. Lawrence Erlbaum Associates, Hillsdale, New Jersey.

Litman, D. J., C. P. Rosé, K. Forbes-Riley, K. VanLehn, D. Bhembe, and S. Silliman. 2006. Spoken versus typed human and computer dialogue tutoring. *International Journal of Artificial Intelligence in Education* 16(2): 145-170.

Purver, M., Kording, K. P., Griffiths, T. L., and Tenenbaum, J. B. 2006. Unsupervised topic modelling for multi-party spoken discourse. *Proceedings of the 21st International Conference on Computational Linguistics and 44th Annual Meeting of the ACL*: 17-24.

Rabiner, L. R. 1989. A tutorial on hidden Markov models and selected applications in speech recognition. *Proceedings of the IEEE* 77(2): 257-286.

Schlegoff, E., and H. Sacks. 1973. Opening up closings. *Semiotica* 7(4): 289-327.

Scott, S. L. 2002. Bayesian methods for hidden Markov models: Recursive computing in the 21st century. *Journal of the American Statistical Association* 97(457): 337-352.

Soller, A., and R. Stevens. 2007. Applications of stochastic analyses for collaborative learning and cognitive assessment. Pages 217-253 in G. R. Hancock, and K. M. Samuelsen, editors. *Advances in latent variable mixture models*. Information Age Publishing.

Tetreault, J. R., and D. J. Litman. 2008. A reinforcement learning approach to evaluating state representations in spoken dialogue systems. *Speech Communication* 50(8-9): 683-696.

VanLehn, K., P. W. Jordan, C. P. Rose, D. Bhembe, M. Bottner, A. Gaydos, M. Makatchev, U. Pappuswamy, M. Ringenberg, and A. Roque. 2002. The architecture of Why2-atlas: A coach for qualitative physics essay writing. *Proceedings of Intelligent Tutoring Systems Conference*: 158–167.

Zinn, C., Moore, J. D., and Core, M. G. 2002. A 3-tier planning architecture for managing tutorial dialogue. *Proceedings of the 6th International Conference on Intelligent Tutoring Systems*: 574-584.

A New Yardstick and Tool for Personalized Vocabulary Building

Thomas K Landauer **Kirill Kireyev** **Charles Panaccione**

Pearson Education,
Knowledge Technologies

{tom.landauer,kirill.kireyev,charles.panaccione}@pearson.com

Abstract

The goal of this research is to increase the value of each individual student's vocabulary by finding words that the student doesn't know, needs to, and is ready to learn. To help identify such words, a better model of how well any given word is expected to be known was created. This is accomplished by using a semantic language model, LSA, to track how every word changes with the addition of more and more text from an appropriate corpus. We define the "maturity" of a word as the degree to which it has become similar to that after training on the entire corpus.

An individual student's average vocabulary level can then be placed on the word-maturity scale by an adaptive test. Finally, the words that the student did or did not know on the test can be used to predict what other words the same student knows by using multiple maturity models trained on random samples of typical educational readings. This detailed information can be used to generate highly customized vocabulary teaching and testing exercises, such as Cloze tests.

1 Introduction

1.1 Why "Vocabulary First"

There are many arguments for the importance of more effective teaching of vocabulary. Here are some examples:

(1) Baker, Simmons, & Kame'enui (1997) found that children who enter school with limited vocabulary knowledge grow much more discrepant over time from their peers who have rich vocabulary knowledge.

(2.) Anderson & Freebody (1981) found that the number of words in student's meaning vocabularies was the best predictor of how well they comprehend text.

(3) An unpublished 1966 study of the correlation between entering scores of Stanford Students on the SAT found the vocabulary component to be the best predictor of grades in every subject, including science.

(4) The number of words students learn varies greatly, from 0.2 to 8 words per day and from 50 to over 3,000 per year. (Anderson & Freebody, 1981)

(5) Printed materials in grades 3 to 9 on average contain almost 90,000, distinct word families and nearly 500,000 word forms (including proper names.) (Nagy & Anderson, 1984).

(6) Nagy and Anderson (1984) found that on average not knowing more than one word in a sentence prevented its tested understanding, and that the probability of learning the meaning of a new word by one encounter on average was less than one in ten.

(7) John B. Carroll's (1993) meta-analysis of factor analyses of measured cognitive ability found the best predictor to be tests of vocabulary.

(8) Hart and Risley's large randomized observational study of the language used in households with young children found that the number of words spoken within hearing of a child was associated with a three-fold difference in vocabulary by school entry.

1.2 The Challenge

Several published sources and inspection of the number of words taught in recent literacy textbooks and online tools suggest that less than 400 words per year are directly tutored in American schools. Thus, the vast majority of vocabulary must be acquired from language exposure, especially from print because the oral vocabulary of daily living is usually estimated to be about 20,000

Proceedings of the NAACL HLT Workshop on Innovative Use of NLP for Building Educational Applications, pages 27–33,
Boulder, Colorado, June 2009.

words, of which most are known by early school years. But it would obviously be of great value to find a way to make the explicit teaching of vocabulary more effective, and to make it multiply the effects of reading. These are the goals of the new methodologies reported here.

It is also clear that words are not learned in isolation: learning the meaning of a new word requires prior knowledge of many other words, and by most estimates it takes a (widely variable) average of ten encounters in different and separated contexts. (This, by the way, is what is required to match human adult competence in the computational language model used here. Given a text corpus highly similar to that experienced by a language learner, the model learns at very close to the same rate as an average child, and it learns new words as much as four times faster the more old words it knows (Landauer & Dumais, 1997).)

An important aside here concerns a widely circulated inference from the Nagy and Anderson (1984) result that teaching words by presenting them in context doesn't produce enough vocabulary growth to be the answer. The problem is that the experiments actually show only that the inserted target word itself is usually not learned well enough to pass a test. But in the simulations, words are learned a little at a time; exposure to a sentence increases the knowledge of many other words, both ones in the sentence and not. Every encounter with any word in context percolates meaning through the whole current and future vocabulary. Indeed, in the simulator, indirect learning is three to five times as much as direct, and is what accounts for its ability to match human vocabulary growth and passage similarity. Put differently, the helpful thing that happens on encountering an unknown word is not guessing its meaning but its contribution to underlying understanding of language.

However, a vicious negative feedback loop lurks in this process. Learning from reading requires vocabulary knowledge. So the vocabulary-rich get richer and the vocabulary-poor get relatively poorer. Fortunately, however, in absolute terms there is a positive feedback loop: the more words you know, the faster you can learn new ones, generating exponential positive growth. Thus the problem and solution may boil down to increasing the growth parameter for a given student enough to make natural reading do its magic better.

Nonetheless, importantly, it is patently obvious that it matters greatly what words are taught how, when and to which students.

The hypothesis, then, is that a set of tools that could determine what particular words an individual student knows and doesn't, and which ones learned (and sentences understood) would most help other words to be learned by that student might have a large multiplying effect. It is such a toolbox that we are endeavoring to create by using a computational language model with demonstrated ability to simulate human vocabulary growth to a reasonably close approximation. The principal foci are better selection and "personalization" of what is taught and teaching more quickly and with more permanence by application of optimal spacing of tests and practice—into which we will not go here.

1.3 Measuring vocabulary knowledge

Currently there are three main methods for measuring learner vocabulary, all of which are inadequate for the goal. They are:

1. Corpus Frequency. Collect a large sample of words used in the domain of interest, for example a collection of textbooks and readers used in classrooms, text from popular newspapers, a large dictionary or the Internet. Rank the words by frequency of occurrence. Test students on a random subset of, say, the 1,000, 2,000 and 5,000 most frequent words, compute the proportion known at each "level" and interpolate and extrapolate. This is a reasonable method, because frequently encountered words are the ones most frequently needed to be understood.
2. Educational Materials. Sample vocabulary lessons and readings over classrooms at different school grades.
3. Expert Judgments. Obtain informed expert opinions about what words are important to know by what age for what purposes.

Some estimates combine two or more of these approaches, and they vary in psychometric sophistication. For example, one of the most sophisticated, the Lexile Framework, uses Rasch scaling (Rasch, 1980) of a large sample of student vocabulary test scores (probability right on a test, holding student ability constant) to create a difficulty measure for sentences and then infers the difficulty of words, in essence, from the average difficulty of the sentences in which they appear.

The problem addressed in the present project goal is that all of these methods measure only the proportion of tested words known at one or more frequency ranges, in chosen school grades or for particular subsets of vocabulary (e.g. "academic" words), and for a very small subset—those tested - some of the words that the majority of a class knows. What they don't measure is exactly which words in the whole corpus a given student knows and to what extent, or which words would be most important for that student to learn.

A lovely analog of the problem comes from Ernst Rothkopf's (1970) metaphor that everyone passes through highly different "word swarms" each day on their way to their (still highly differentiated) adult literacy.

2 A new metric: Word Maturity

The new metric first applies Latent Semantic Analysis (LSA) to model how representation of individual words changes and grows toward their adult meaning as more and more language is encountered. Once the simulation has been created, an adaptive testing method can be applied to place individual words on separate growth curves - characteristic functions in psychometric terminology. Finally, correlations between growth curves at given levels can be used to estimate the achieved growth of other words.

2.1 How it works in more detail: LSA.

A short review of how LSA works will be useful here because it is often misunderstood and a correct interpretation is important in what follows. LSA models how words combine into meaningful passages, the aspect of verbal meaning we take to be most critical to the role of words in literacy. It does this by assuming that the "meaning" (please bear with the nickname) of a meaningful passage is the sum of the meanings of its words:

```
Meaning of passage =
 {meaning of first wd} +
 {meaning of second word} + …  +
 {meaning of last word}
```

A very large and representative corpus of the language to be modeled is first collected and represented as a term-by-document matrix. A powerful matrix algebra method called Singular Value Decomposition is then used to make every paragraph in the corpus conform to the above objective function—word representations sum to passage representations - up to a best least-squares approximation. A dimensionality-reduction step is performed, resulting in each word and passage meanings represented as a (typically) 300 element real number vector. Note that the property of a vector standing for a word form in this representation is the effect that it has on the vector standing for the passage. (In particular, it is only indirectly a reflection of how similar two words are to each other or how frequently they have occurred in the same passages.) In the result, the vector for a word is the average of the vectors for all the passages in which it occurs, and the vector for a passage is, of course, the average all of its words.

In many previous applications to education, including automatic scoring of essays, the model's similarity to human judgments (e.g. by mutual information measures) has been found to be 80 to 90% as high as that between two expert humans, and, as mentioned earlier, the rate at which it learns the meaning of words as assessed by various standardized and textbook-based tests has been found to closely match that of students. For more details, evaluations and previous educational applications, see (Landauer et al., 2007).

2.2 How it works in more detail: Word Maturity.

Taking LSA to be a sufficiently good approximation of human learning of the meanings conveyed by printed word forms, we can use it to track their gradual acquisition as a function of increasing exposure to text representative in size and content of that which students at successive grade levels read.

Thus, to model the growth of meaning of individual words, a series of sequentially accumulated LSA "semantic spaces" (the collection of vectors for all of the words and passages) are created. Cumulative portions of the corpus thus emulate the growing total amount of text that has been read by a student. At each step, a new LSA semantic space is created from a cumulatively larger subset of the full adult corpus.

Several different ways of choosing the successive sets of passages to be added to the training set have been tried, ranging from ones based on readability metrics (such as Lexiles or DRPs) to entirely randomly selected subsets. Here, the steps are based on Lexiles to emulate their order of encounter in typical school reading.

This process results in a separate LSA model of word meanings corresponding to each stage of language learning. To determine how well a word or passage is known at a given stage of learning—a given number or proportion of passages from the corpus—its vector in the LSA model corresponding to a particular stage is compared with the vector of the full adult model (one that has been trained on a corpus corresponding to a typical adult's amount of language exposure). This is done using a linear transformation technique known as Procrustes Alignment to align the two spaces—those after a given step to those based on the full corpus, which we call its "adult" meaning.

Word *maturity* is defined as the similarity of a word's vector at a given stage of training and that at its adult stage as measured by cosine. It is scaled as values ranging between 0 (least mature) and 1 (most mature).

Figure 1 shows growth curves for an illustrative set of words. In this example, 17 successive cumulative steps were created, each containing ~5000 additional passages.

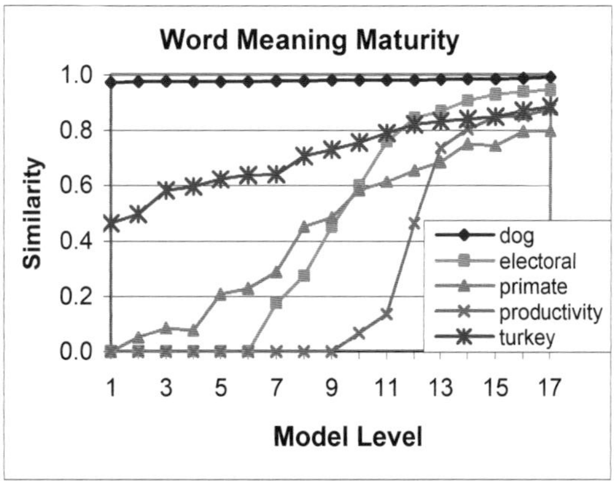

Figure 1. An illustration of meaning maturity growth of several words as a function of language exposure.

Some words (e.g. "dog") are almost at their adult meaning very early. Others hardly get started until later. Some grow quickly, some slowly. Some grow smoothly, some in spurts. Some, like "turkey," grow rapidly, plateau, then resume growing again, presumably due to multiple senses ("Thanksgiving bird" vs. "country") learned at different periods (in LSA, multiple "senses" are combined in a word representation approximately in proportion to their frequency.)

The maturity metric has several conceptual advantages over existing measures of the status of a word's meaning, and in particular should be kept conceptually distinct from the ambiguous and often poorly defined term "difficulty" and from whether or not students in general or at some developmental stage can properly use, define or understand its meaning. It is a mathematical property of a word that may or may not be related to what particular people can do with it.

What it does is provide a detailed view of the course of development of a word's changing representation—its "meaning", reciprocally defined as its effect on the "meaning" of passages in which it occurs,—as a function of the amount and nature of the attestedly meaningful passages in which it has been encountered. Its relation to "difficulty" as commonly used would depend, among other things, on whether a human could use it <u>for some purpose</u> at <u>some stage of development of the word</u>. Thus, its relation to a student's use of a word requires a second step of aligning the student's word knowledge with the metric scaling. This is analogous to describing a runner's "performance" by aligning it with well-defined metrics for time and distance.

It is nevertheless worth noting that the word maturity metric is not based directly on corpus frequency as some other measures of word status are (although its average level over all maturities is moderately highly correlated with total corpus frequency as it should be) or on other heuristics, such as grade of first use or expert opinions of suitability.

What is especially apparent in the graph above is that after a given amount of language exposure, analogous to age or school grade, there are large differences in the maturity of different words. In fact the correlation between frequency of occurrence in a particular one of the 17 intermediate corpora and word maturity is only 0.1, measured over 20,000 random words. According to the model--and surely common sense--words of the same frequency of encounter (or occurrence in a corpus) are far from equally well known. Thus, all methods for "leveling" text and vocabulary instruction based on word frequency must hide a great range of differences.

To illustrate this in more detail, Table 1, shows computed word maturities for a set of words that have nearly the same frequency in the full corpus (column *four*) when they have been added only 50±5 times *(column two)*. The differences are so large as to suggest the choice of words to teach students in a given school grade would profit much from being based on something more discriminative than either average word frequency or word frequency as found in the texts being read or in the small sample that can be humanly judged. Even better, it would appear, should be to base what is taught to a given student on what that student does and doesn't know but needs to locally and would most profit from generally.

Word	Occurrences in intermediate corpus (level 5)	Occurrences in adult corpus	Word maturity (at level 5)
marble	54	485	0.21
sunshine	49	508	0.31
drugs	53	532	0.42
carpet	48	539	0.59
twin	48	458	0.61
earn	53	489	0.70
beam	47	452	0.76

Table 1 A sample of words with roughly the same number of occurrences in both intermediate (~50) and adult (~500) corpus

The word maturity metric appears to perform well when validated by some external methods. For example, it reliably discriminates between words that were assigned to be taught in different school grades by (Biemiller, 2008), based on a combination of expert judgments and comprehension tests ($p < 0.03$), as shown in Table 2.

grade 2, known by > 80%	grade 2, known by 40-80%	grade 6, known by 40-80%	grade 6, known by < 40%
n=1034	n=606	n=1125	n=1411
4.4	**6.5**	**8.8**	**9.5**

Table 2 Average level for each word to reach a 0.5 maturity threshold, for words that are known at different levels by students of different grades (Biemiller, 2008).

Median word maturity also tracks the differences ($p < 0.01$) between essays written by students in different grades as shown in Figure 2.

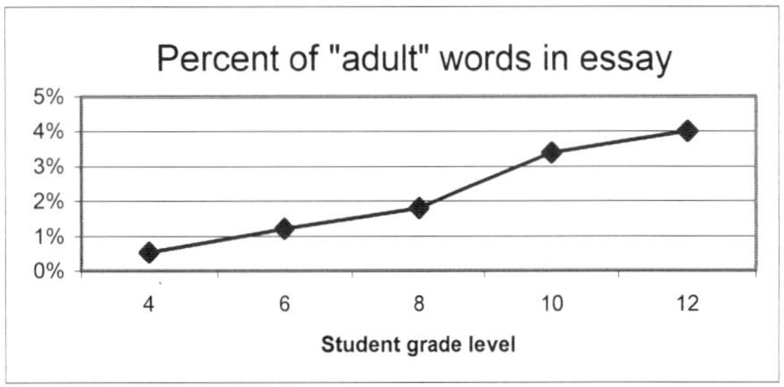

Figure 2 Percentage of "adult" words used in essays written by students of different grade levels. "Adult" words are defined as words that reach a 0.5 word maturity threshold at or later than the point where half of the words in the language have reached 0.5 threshold.

2.3 Finding words to teach individual students

Using the computed word maturity values, a sigmoid characteristic curve is generated to approximate the growth curve of every word in the corpus. A model similar to one used in item response theory (Rasch, 1980) can be constructed from the growth curve due to its similarity in shape and function to an IRT characteristic curve; both curves represent the ability of a student. The characteristic curve for the IRT is needed to properly administer adaptive testing, which greatly increases the precision and generalizeability of the exam. Words to be tested are chosen from the corpus beginning at the average maturity of words at the approximate grade level of the student. Thirty to fifty word tests are used to home in on the student's average word maturity level. In initial trials, a combination of yes/no and Cloze tests are being used. Because our model does not treat all words of a given frequency as equivalent, this alone supports a more precise and personalized measure of a student's vocabulary. In plan, the student level will be updated by the results of additional tests administered in school or by Internet delivery.

The final step is to generalize from the assessed knowledge of words a particular student (let's call her Alice) is tested on to other words in the corpus. This is accomplished by first generating a large number of simulated students (and their word maturity curves) using the method described above. Each simulated student is trained on one of many ~ 12 million word corpora, size and content approximating the lifelong reading of a typical college student, that have been randomly sampled from a representative corpus of more than half a billion words. Some of these simulated students' knowledge of the words being tested will be more similar to Alice than others. We can then estimate Alice's knowledge of any other word *w* in the corpus by averaging the levels of knowledge of *w* by simulated students whose patterns of tested word knowledge are most similar hers. The method rests on the assumption that there are sufficiently strong correlations between the words that a given student has learned at a given stage (e.g. resulting from Rothkopf's personal "swarms'.) While simulations are promising, empirical evidence as to the power of the approach with non-simulated students is yet to be determined.

3 Applying the method

On the assumption that learning words by their effects on passage meanings as LSA does is good, initial applications use Cloze items to simultaneously test and teach word meanings by presenting them in a natural linguistic context. Using the simulator, the context words in an item are predicted to be ones that the individual student already knows at a chosen level. The target words, where the wider pedagogy permits, are ones that are related and important to the meaning of the sentence or passage, as measured by LSA cosine similarity metric, and, ipso facto, the context tends to contextually teach their meaning. They can also be chosen to be those that are computationally estimated to be the most important for a student to know in order to comprehend assigned or student-chosen readings—because their lack has the most effect on passage meanings—and/or in the language in general. Using a set of natural language processing algorithms (such as n-gram models, POS-tagging, WordNet relations and LSA) the distracter items for each Cloze are chosen in such a way that they are appropriate grammatically, but not semantically, as illustrated in the example below.

In summary, Cloze-test generation involves the following steps:

1. Determine the student's overall knowledge level and individual word knowledge predictions based on previous interactions.

2. Find important words in a reading that are appropriate for a particular student (using metrics that include word maturity).

3. For each word, find a sentence in a large collection of natural text, such that the rest of the sentence semantically implies (is related to) the target word and is appropriate for student's knowledge level.

4. Find distracter words that are (a) level-appropriate, (b) are sufficiently related and (c) fit grammatically, but (d) not semantically, into the sentence.

All the living and nonliving things around an ___ is its environment. A. organism B. oxygen C. algae
Freshwater habitats can be classified according to the characteristic species of fish found in them, indicating the strong ecological relationship between an ___ and its environment. A. adaptation B. energy C. organism

Table 3 Examples of auto-generated Cloze tests for the same word (*organism*) and two students of lower and higher ability, respectively.

4 Summary and present status

A method based on computational modeling of language, in particular one that makes the representation of the meaning of a word its effect on the meaning of a passage its objective, LSA, has been developed and used to simulate the growth of meaning of individual word representations towards those of literate adults. Based thereon, a new metric for word meaning growth called "Word Maturity" is proposed. The measure is then applied to adaptively measuring the average level of an individual student's vocabulary, presumably with greater breadth and precision than offered by other methods, especially those based on knowledge of words at different corpus frequency. There are many other things the metric may support, for example better personalized measurement of text comprehensibility.

However, it must be emphasized that the method is very new and essentially untried except in simulation. And it is worth noting that while the proposed method is based on LSA, many or all of its functionalities could be obtained with some other computational language models, for example the Topics model. Comparisons with other methods will be of interest, and more and more rigorous evaluations are needed, as are trials with more various applications to assure robustness.

5 References

Richard C. Anderson, Peter Freebody. 1981. *Vocabulary Knowledge.* In J. T. Guthrie (Ed.), *Comprehension and teaching: Research reviews* (pp. 77-117). International Reading Association, Newark DE.

Scott K. Baker, Deborah C. Simmons, Edward J. Kameenui. 1997. *Vocabulary acquisition: Research bases.* In Simmons, D. C. & Kameenui, E. J. (Eds.), *What reading research tells us about children with diverse learning needs: Bases and basics.* Erlbaum, Mahwah, NJ.

Andrew Biemiller (2008). Words Worth Teaching. Co-lumbus, OH: SRA/McGraw-Hill.

John B Carroll. 1993. *Cognitive Abilities: A survey of factor-analytic studies.* Cambridge: Cambridge University Press, *1993.*

Betty Hart, Todd R. Risley. 1995. *Meaningful differences in the everyday experience of young American children.* Brookes Publishing, 1995.

Melanie R. Kuhn, Steven A. Stahl. 1998. *Teaching children to learn word meanings from context: A synthesis and some questions.* Journal of Literacy Research, 30(1) 119-138.

Thomas K Landauer, Susan Dumais. 1997. *A solution to Plato's problem: The Latent Semantic Analysis theory of the Acquisition, Induction, and Representation of Knowledge.* Psychological Review, 104, pp 211-240.

Thomas K Landauer, Danielle S. McNamara, Simon Dennis, and Walter Kintsch. 2007. *Handbook of Latent Semantic Analysis.* Lawrence Erlbaum.

Cleborne D. Maddux (1999). Peabody Picture Vocabulary Test III (PPVT-III). Diagnostique, v24 n1-4, p221-28, 1998-1999

William E. Nagy, Richard C. Anderson. 1984. *How many words are there in printed school English?* Reading Research Quarterly, 19, 304-330.

Ernst Z. Rothkopf, Ronald D. Thurner. 1970. *Effects of written instructional material on the statistical structure of test essays.* Journal of Educacational Psychology, 61, 83-89.

George Rasch. (1980). *Probabilistic models for some intelligence and attainment tests.* (Copenhagen, Danish Institute for Educational Research), expanded edition (1980) with foreword and afterword by B.D. Wright. Chicago: The University of Chicago Press.

Supporting the Adaptation of Texts for Poor Literacy Readers: a Text Simplification Editor for Brazilian Portuguese

Arnaldo Candido Jr., Erick Maziero, Caroline Gasperin, Thiago A. S. Pardo, Lucia Specia, and Sandra M. Aluisio

Center of Computational Linguistics (NILC) / Department of Computer Sciences, University of São Paulo
Av. Trabalhador São-Carlense, 400. 13560-970 - São Carlos/SP, Brazil
arnaldoc@icmc.usp.br, egmaziero@gmail.com, {cgasperin,taspardo,lspecia,sandra}@icmc.usp.br

Abstract

In this paper we investigate the task of text simplification for Brazilian Portuguese. Our purpose is three-fold: to introduce a simplification tool for such language and its underlying development methodology, to present an on-line authoring system of simplified text based on the previous tool, and finally to discuss the potentialities of such technology for education. The resources and tools we present are new for Portuguese and innovative in many aspects with respect to previous initiatives for other languages.

1 Introduction

In Brazil, according to the index used to measure the literacy level of the population (INAF - National Indicator of Functional Literacy), a vast number of people belong to the so called rudimentary and basic literacy levels. These people are only able to find explicit information in short texts (rudimentary level) or process slightly longer texts and make simple inferences (basic level). INAF reports that 68% of the 30.6 million Brazilians between 15 and 64 years who have studied up to 4 years remain at the rudimentary literacy level, and 75% of the 31.1 million who studied up to 8 years remain at the rudimentary or basic levels.

Reading comprehension entails three elements: the reader who is meant to comprehend; the text that is to be comprehended and the activity in which comprehension is a part of (Snow, 2002). In addition to the content presented in the text, the vocabulary load of the text and its linguistic structure, discourse style, and genre interact with the reader's knowledge. When these factors do not match the reader's knowledge and experience, the text becomes too complex for the comprehension to occur. In this paper we will focus on the text and the aspects of it that make reading difficult or easy. One solution to ease the syntactic structure of a text is via Text Simplification (TS) facilities.

TS aims to maximize the comprehension of written texts through the simplification of their linguistic structure. This may involve simplifying lexical and syntactic phenomena, by substituting words that are only understood by a few people with words that are more usual, and by breaking down and changing the syntactic structure of the sentence, respectively. As a result, it is expected that the text can be more easily understood both by humans and computer systems (Mapleson, 2006; Siddharthan, 2003, Max, 2006). TS may also involve dropping parts or full sentences and adding some extra material to explain a difficult point. This is the case, for example, of the approach presented by Petersen and Ostendorf (2007), in which abridged versions of articles are used in adult literacy learning.

It has already been shown that long sentences, conjoined sentences, embedded clauses, passives, non-canonical word order, and use of low-frequency words, among other things, increase text complexity for language-impaired readers (Siddharthan, 2002; Klebanov et al., 2004; Devlin and Unthank, 2006). The Plain English initiative makes available guidelines to make texts easier to comprehend: the *Plain Language*[1]. In principle, its recommendations can be applied to any language. Although some of them are directly useful for TS systems (e.g., subject-verb-object order and active voice), others are difficult to specify (e.g., how simple each syntactic construction is and which words are simple).

In this paper we present the results of a study of syntactic simplification for Brazilian Portuguese (BP) and a rule-based syntactic simplification system for this language that was developed based on this study – the first of this kind for BP. We also present an on-line authoring tool for creating simplified texts. One possible application of this tool is to help teachers to produce instructional texts

[1] http://www.plainlanguage.gov

Proceedings of the NAACL HLT Workshop on Innovative Use of NLP for Building Educational Applications, pages 34–42, Boulder, Colorado, June 2009.

to be used in classrooms. The study is part of the PorSimples project[2] (Simplification of Portuguese Text for Digital Inclusion and Accessibility), which aims at producing text simplification tools for promoting digital inclusion and accessibility for people with different levels of literacy, and possibly other kinds of reading disabilities.

This paper is organized as follows. In Section 2 we present related approaches for text simplification with educational purposes. In Section 3 we describe the proposed approach for syntactic simplification, which is used within an authoring tool described in Section 4. In Section 5 we discuss possible uses of text simplification for educational purposes.

2 Related work

Burstein (2009) presents an NLP-based application for educational purposes, named Text Adaptor, which resembles our authoring tool. It includes complex sentence highlighting, text elaboration (word substitutions by easier ones), text summarization and translation. The system does not perform syntactic simplification, but simply suggests, using a shallow parser, that some sentences might be too complex. Specific hints on the actual source of complexity are not provided.

Petersen (2007) addresses the task of text simplification in the context of second-language learning. A data-driven approach to simplification is proposed using a corpus of paired articles in which each original sentence does not necessarily have a corresponding simplified sentence, making it possible to learn where writers have dropped or simplified sentences. A classifier is used to select the sentences to simplify, and Siddharthan's syntactic simplification system (Siddharthan, 2003) is used to split the selected sentences. In our approach, we do not drop sentences, since we believe that all the content must be kept in the text.

Siddharthan proposes a syntactic simplification architecture that relies on shallow text analysis and favors time performance. The general goal of the architecture is to make texts more accessible to a broader audience; it has not targeted any particular application. The system treats apposition, relative clauses, coordination and subordination. Our method, on the other hand, relies on deep parsing (Bick, 2000). We treat the same phenomena as Siddharthan, but also deal with Subject-Verb-Object ordering (in Portuguese sentences can be written in different orders) and passive to active voice conversion. Siddharthan's system deals with non-finite clauses which are not handled by our system at this stage.

Lal and Ruger's (2002) created a bayesian summarizer with a built-in lexical simplification module, based on WordNet and MRC psycho-linguistic database[3]. The system focuses on schoolchildren and provides background information about people and locations in the text, which are retrieved from databases. Our rule-based simplification system only replaces discourse markers for more common ones using lexical resources built in our project, instead of inserting additional information in the text.

Max (2005, 2006) applies text simplification in the writing process by embedding an interactive text simplification system into a word processor. At the user's request, an automatic parser analyzes an individual sentence and the system applies handcrafted rewriting rules. The resulting suggested simplifications are ranked by a score of syntactic complexity and potential change of meaning. The writer then chooses their preferred simplification. This system ensures accurate output, but requires human intervention at every step. Our system, on the other hand, is autonomous, even though the user is able to undo any undesirable simplification or to choose alternative simplifications. These alternative simplifications may be produced in two cases: i) to compose a new subject in simplifications involving relatives and appositions and ii) to choose among one of the coordinate or subordinate simplifications when there is ambiguity regarding to conjunctions.

Inui et al. (2003) proposes a rule-based system for text simplification aimed at deaf people. The authors create readability assessments based on questionnaires answered by teachers about the deaf. With approximately one thousand manually created rules, the authors generate several paraphrases for each sentence and train a classifier to select the simpler ones. Promising results are obtained, although different types of errors on the paraphrase generation are encountered, such as problems with verb conjugation and regency. In our work we produce alternative simplifications only in the two cases explained above.

[2] http://caravelas.icmc.usp.br/wiki/index.php/Principal

[3] http://www.psych.rl.ac.uk/

Caseli et al. (2009) developed an annotation editor to support the building of parallel corpora of original and simplified texts in Brazilian Portuguese. The tool was used to build a corpus of simplified texts aimed at people with rudimentary and basic literacy levels. We have used the parallel corpus to evaluate our rule-based simplification system. The on-line authoring system presented in this paper evolved from this annotation editor.

There are also commercial systems like Simplus[4] and StyleWriter[5], which aim to support Plain English writing.

3 A rule-based syntactic simplification system

Our text simplification system comprises seven operations (see Sections 3.1 and 3.2), which are applied to a text in order to make its syntactic structure simpler. These operations are applied sentence by sentence, following the 3-stage architecture proposed by Siddharthan (2002), which includes stages of analysis, transformation and regeneration. In Siddharthan's work, the analysis stage performs the necessary linguistic analyses of the input sentences, such as POS tagging and chunking; the transformation stage applies simplification rules, producing simplified versions of the sentences; the regeneration stage performs operations on the simplified sentences to make them readable, like referring expressions generation, cue words rearrangement, and sentence ordering. Differently from such architecture, currently our regeneration stage only includes the treatment of cue words and a surface forms (GSF) generator, which is used to adjust the verb conjugation and regency after some simplification operations.

As a single sentence may contain more than one complex linguistic phenomenon, simplification operations are applied in cascade to a sentence, as described in what follows.

3.1 Simplification cases and operations

As result of a study on which linguistic phenomena make BP text complex to read and how these phenomena could be simplified, we elaborated a manual of BP syntactic simplification (Aluisio et al., 2008). The rule-based text simplification system developed here is based on the specifications in this manual. According to this manual, simplification operations should be applied when any of the 22 linguistic phenomena presented in Table 1 is detected.

The possible operations suggested to be applied in order to simplify these phenomena are: (a) split the sentence, (b) change a discourse marker by a simpler and/or more frequent one (the indication is to avoid the ambiguous ones), (c) change passive to active voice, (d) invert the order of the clauses, (e) convert to subject-verb-object ordering, (f) change topicalization and detopicalization of adverbial phrases and (g) non-simplification.

Table 1 shows the list of all simplification phenomena covered by our manual, the clues used to identify the phenomena, the simplification operations that should be applied in each case, the expected order of clauses in the resulting sentence, and the cue phrases (translated here from Portuguese) used to replace complex discourse markers or to glue two sentences. In column 2, we consider the following clues: syntactic information (S), punctuation (P), and lexicalized clues, such as conjunctions (Cj), relative pronouns (Pr) and discourse markers (M), and semantic information (Sm, and NE for named entities).

3.2 Identifying simplification cases and applying simplification rules

Each sentence is parsed in order to identify cases for simplification. We use parser PALAVRAS (Bick, 2000) for Portuguese. This parser provides lexical information (morphology, lemma, part-of-speech, and semantic information) and the syntactic trees for each sentence. For some operations, surface information (such as punctuation or lexicalized cue phrases) is used to identify the simplification cases, as well as to assist simplification process. For example, to detect and simplify subjective non-restrictive relative clauses (where the relative pronoun is the subject of the relative clause), the following steps are performed:

1. The presence of a relative pronoun is verified.
2. Punctuation is verified in order to distinguish it from restrictive relative clauses: check if the pronoun occurs after a comma or semicolon.
3. Based on the position of the pronoun, the next punctuation symbol is searched to define the boundaries of the relative clause.

[4] http://www.linguatechnologies.com/english/home.html
[5] http://www.editorsoftware.com/writing-software

4. The first part of the simplified text is generated, consisting of the original sentence without the embedded relative clause.
5. The noun phrase in the original sentence to which the relative clause refers is identified.
6. A second simplified sentence is generated, consisting of the noun phrase (as subject) and the relative clause (without the pronoun).

The identification of the phenomena and the application of the operations are prone to errors though. Some of the clues that indicate the occurrence of the phenomena may be ambiguous. For example, some of the discourse markers that are used to identify subordinate clauses can indicate more than one type of these: for instance, "como" (in English "like", "how" or "as") can indicate reason, conformative or concessive subordinate clauses. Since there is no other clue that can help us disambiguate among those, we always select the case that occurs more frequently according to a corpus study of discourse markers and the rhetoric relations that they entitle (Pardo and Nunes, 2008). However, we can also treat all cases and let the user decide the simplifications that is most appropriate.

Phenomenon	*Clues*	*Op*	*Clause Order*	*Cue phrase*	*Comments*
1.Passive voice	S	c			Verb may have to be adapted
2.Embedded appositive	S	a	Original/ App.		Appositive: Subject is the head of original + to be in present tense + apposition
3.Asyndetic coordinate clause	S	a	Keep order		New sentences: Subjects are the head of the original subject
4.Additive coordinate clause	S, Cj	a	Keep order	Keep marker	Marker appears in the beginning of the new sentence
5.Adversative coordinate clause	M	a, b	Keep order	*But*	
6.Correlated coordinate clause	M	a, b	Keep order	*Also*	Original markers disappear
7.Result coordinate clause	S, M	a, b	Keep order	*As a result*	
8.Reason coordinate clause	S, M	a, b	Keep order	*This happens because*	May need some changes in verb
9.Reason subordinate clause	M	a, b, d	Sub/Main	*With this*	To keep the ordering cause, result
10.Comparative subordinate clause	M	a, b	Main/Sub	*Also*	Rule for *such ... as, so ... as* markers
	M	g			Rule for the other markers or short sentences
11.Concessive subordinate clause	M	a, b, d	Sub/Main	*But*	"Clause 1 *although* clause 2" is changed to "Clause 2. *But* clause 1"
	M	a, b	Main/Sub	*This happens even if*	Rule for hypothetical sentences
12.Conditional subordinate clause	S, M	d	Sub/Main		Pervasive use in simple accounts
13. Result subordinate clause	M	a, b	Main/Sub	*Thus*	May need some changes in verb
14.Final/Purpose subordinate clause	S, M	a, b	Main/Sub	*The goal is*	
15.Confirmative subordinate clause	M	a, b, d	Sub/Main	*Confirms that*	May need some changes in verb
16.Time subordinate clause	M	a	Sub/Main		May need some changes in verb
	M	a, b		*Then*	Rule for markers: after that, as soon as
17. Proportional Subordinate Clause	M	g			
18. Non-finite subordinate clause	S	g			
19.Non-restrictive relative clause	S, P, Pr	a	Original/ Relative		Relative: Subject is the head of original + relative (subjective relative clause)
20.Restrictive relative clause	S, Pr	a	Relative/ Original		Relative: Subject is the head of original + relative (subjective relative clause)
21.Non Subject-Verb-Object order	S	e			Rewrite in Subject-Verb-Object order
22. Adverbial phrases in theme position	S, NE, Sm	f	In study		In study

Table 1: Cases, operations, order and cue phrases

Every phenomenon has one or more simplification steps associated with it, which are applied to perform the simplification operations. Below we detail each operation and discuss the challenges involved and our current limitations in their implementing.

a) Splitting the sentence - This operation is the most frequent one. It requires finding the split point in the original sentence (such as the boundaries of relative clauses and appositions, the position of coordinate or subordinate conjunctions) and the creation of a new sentence, whose subject corresponds to the replication of a noun phrase in the original sentence. This operation increases the text length, but decreases the length of the sentences. With the duplication of the term from the original sentence (as subject of the new sentence), the resulting text contains redundant information, but it is very helpful for people at the rudimentary literacy level.

When splitting sentences due to the presence of apposition, we need to choose the element in the original sentence to which it is referring, so that this element can be the subject of the new sentence. At the moment we analyze all NPs that precede the apposition and check for gender and number agreement. If more than one candidate passes the agreement test, we choose the closest one among these; if none does, we choose the closest among all candidates. In both cases we can also pass the decision on to the user, which we do in our authoring tool described in Section 4.

For treating relative clauses we have the same problem as for apposition (finding the NP to which the relative clause is anchored) and an additional one: we need to choose if the referent found should be considered the subject or the object of the new sentence. Currently, the parser indicates the syntactic function of the relative pronoun and that serves as a clue.

b) Changing discourse marker - In most cases of subordination and coordination, discourse markers are replaced by most commonly used ones, which are more easily understood. The selection of discourse markers to be replaced and the choice of new markers (shown in Table 1, col. 4) are done based on the study of Pardo and Nunes (2008).

c) Transformation to active voice - Clauses in the passive voice are turned into active voice, with the reordering of the elements in the clause and the modification of the tense and form of the verb. Any other phrases attached to the object of the original sentence have to be carried with it when it moves to the subject position, since the voice changing operation is the first to be performed. For instance, the sentence:

> "More than 20 people have been bitten by gold piranhas (Serrasalmus Spilopleura), which live in the waters of the Sanchuri dam, next to the BR-720 highway, 40 km from the city."

is simplified to:

> "Gold piranhas (Serrasalmus Spilopleura), which live in the waters of the Sanchuri dam, next to the BR-720 highway, 40 km from the city, have bitten more than 20 people."

After simplification of the relative clause and apposition, the final sentence is:

> "Gold piranhas have bitten more than 20 people. Gold piranhas live in the waters of the Sanchuri dam, next to the BR-720 highway, 40 km from the city. Gold piranhas are Serrasalmus Spilopleura."

d) Inversion of clause ordering - This operation was primarily designed to handle subordinate clauses, by moving the main clause to the beginning of the sentence, in order to help the reader processing it on their working memory (Graesser et al., 2004). Each of the subordination cases has a more appropriate order for main and subordinate clauses (as shown in Table 1, col. 3), so that "independent" information is placed before the information that depends on it. In the case of concessive subordinate clauses, for example, the subordinate clause is placed before the main clause. This gives the sentence a logical order of the expressed ideas. See the example below, in which there is also a change of discourse marker and sentence splitting, all operations assigned to concessive subordinate clauses:

> "The building hosting the Brazilian Consulate was also evacuated, although the diplomats have obtained permission to carry on working."

Its simplified version becomes:

> "The diplomats have obtained permission to carry on working. But the building hosting the Brazilian Consulate was also evacuated."

e) Subject-Verb-Object ordering - If a sentence is not in the form of subject-verb-object, it should be rearranged. This operation is based only on information from the syntactic parser. The example below shows a case in which the subject is after the verb (translated literally from Portuguese, preserving the order of the elements):

> "On the 9th of November of 1989, fell the wall that for almost three decades divided Germany."

Its simplified version is:

> "On the 9th of November of 1989, the wall that for almost three decades divided Germany fell."

Currently the only case we are treating is the non-canonical order Verb-Object-Subject. We plan to treat other non-canonical orderings in the near future. Besides that, we still have to define how to deal with elliptic subjects and impersonal verbs (which in Portuguese do not require a subject).

When performing this operation and the previous one, a generator of surface forms (GSF) is used to adjust the verb conjugation and regency. The GSF is compiled from the Apertium morphological dictionaries enhanced with the entries of Unitex-BP (Muniz et al., 2005), with an extra processing to map the tags of the parser to those existing in morphological dictionaries (Caseli et al., 2007) to obtain an adjusted verb in the modified sentence.

f) Topicalization and detopicalization - This operation is used to topicalize or detopicalize an adverbial phrase. We have not implemented this operation yet, but have observed that moving adverbial phrases to the end or to the front of sentences can make them simpler in some cases. For instance, the sentence in the last example would become:

"The wall that for almost three decades divided Germany fell on the 9th of November of 1989."

We are still investigating how this operation could be applied, that is, which situations require (de)topicalization.

3.3 The cascaded application of the rules

As previously mentioned, one sentence may contain several phenomena that could be simplified, and we established the order in which they are treated. The first phenomenon to be treated is passive voice. Secondly, embedded appositive clauses are resolved, since they are easy to simplify and less prone to errors. Thirdly, subordinate, non-restrictive and restrictive relative clauses are treated, and only then the coordinate clauses are dealt with.

As the rules were designed to treat each case individually, it is necessary to apply the operations in cascade, in order to complete the simplification process for each sentence. At each iteration, we (1) verify the phenomenon to be simplified following the standard order indicated above; (2) when a phenomenon is identified, its simplification is executed; and (3) the resulting simplified sentence goes through a new iteration. This process continues until there are no more phenomena. The cascade nature of the process is crucial because the simplified sentence presents a new syntactic structure and needs to be reparsed, so that the further simplification operations can be properly applied. However, this process consumes time and is considered the bottleneck of the system.

3.4 Simplification evaluation

We have so far evaluated the capacity of our rule-based simplifier to identify the phenomena present in each sentence, and to recommend the correct simplification operation. We compared the operations recommended by the system with the ones performed manually by an annotator in a corpus of 104 news articles from the Zero Hora newspaper, which can be seen in our Portal of Parallel Corpora of Simplified Texts[6]. Table 2 presents the number of occurrences of each simplification operation in this corpus.

Simplification Operations	*# Sentences*
Non-simplification	2638
Subject-verb-object ordering	44
Transformation to active voice	154
Inversion of clause ordering	265
Splitting sentences	1103

Table 2. Statistics on the simplification operations

The performance of the system for this task is presented in Table 3 in terms of precision, recall, and F-measure for each simplification operation.

Operation	*P*	*R*	*F*
Splitting sentences	64.07	82.63	72.17
Inversion of clause ordering	15.40	18.91	16.97
Transformation to active voice	44.29	44.00	44.14
Subject-verb-object ordering	1.12	4.65	1.81
ALL	51.64	65.19	57.62
Non-simplification	64.69	53.58	58.61

Table 3. Performance on defining simplification operations according to syntactic phenomena

These results are preliminary, since we are still refining our rules. Most of the recall errors on the inversion of clause ordering are due to the absence of a few discourse markers in the list of markers that we use to identify such cases. The majority of recall errors on sentence splitting are due to mistakes on the output of the syntactic parser and to the number of ordering cases considered and implemented so far. The poor performance for subject-verb-object ordering, despite suffering from mistakes of the parser, indicates that our rules for this operation need to be refined. The same applies to inversion of clause ordering.

We did not report performance scores related to the "changing discourse marker" operation because in our evaluation corpus this operation is merged with other types of lexical substitution. However, in

[6] http://caravelas.icmc.usp.br/portal/index.php

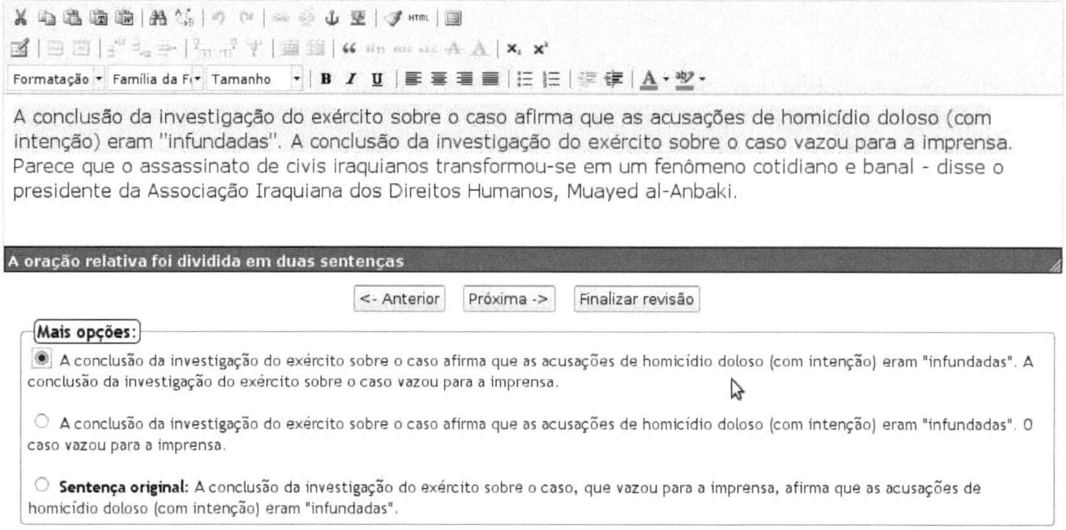

Figure 1: Interface of the *Simplifica* system

order to assess if the sentences were correctly simplified, it is necessary to do a manual evaluation, since it is not possible to automatically compare the output of the rule-based simplifier with the annotated corpus, as the sentences in the corpus have gone through operations that are not performed by the simplifier (such as lexical substitution). We are in the process of performing such manual evaluation.

4 *Simplifica* editor: supporting authors

We developed *Simplifica*[7] (Figure 1), an authoring system to help writers to produce simplified texts. It employs the simplification technology described in the previous section. It is a web-based WYSIWYG editor, based on TinyMCE web editor[8].

The user inputs a text in the editor, customizes the simplification settings where one or more simplifications can be chosen to be applied in the text and click on the "simplify" button. This triggers the syntactic simplification system, which returns an XML file containing the resulting text and tags indicating the performed simplification operations. After that, the simplified version of the text is shown to the user, and he/she can revise the automatic simplification.

4.1 The XML representation of simplification operations

Our simplification system generates an XML file describing all simplification operations applied to a text. This file can be easily parsed using standard XML parsers. Table 5 presents the XML annotation to the "gold piranhas" example in Section 3.2.

```
<simplification type="passive">
  <simplification type="appositive">
    <simplification type="relative">
      Gold piranhas have bitten more than 20 people. Gold
      piranhas live in the waters of the Sanchuri dam, next to
      the BR-720 highway, 40 km from the city.
    </simplification>
    Gold piranhas are Serrasalmus Spilopleura.
  </simplification>
</simplification>
```

Table 5. XML representation of a simplified text

In our annotation, each sentence receives a <simplification> tag which describes the simplified phenomena (if any); sentences that did not need simplification are indicated with a <simplification type="no"> tag. The other simplification types refer to the eighteen simplification cases presented in Table 1. Nested tags indicate multiple operations applied to the same sentence.

4.2 Revising the automatic simplification

Once the automatic simplification is done, a review screen shows the user the simplified text so that he/she can visualize all the modifications applied and approve or reject them, or select alternative simplifications. Figure 1 shows the reviewing screen and a message related to the simplification performed below the text simplified.

The user can revise simplified sentences one at a time; the selected sentence is automatically highlighted. The user can accept or reject a

[7] http://www.nilc.icmc.usp.br/porsimples/simplifica/
[8] http://tinymce.moxiecode.com/

simplified sentence using the buttons below the text. In the beginning of the screen "Mais opções", alternative simplifications for the sentence are shown: this facility gives the user the possibility to resolve cases known to be ambiguous (as detailed in Sections 2 and 3.2) for which the automatic simplification may have made a mistake. In the bottom of the same screen we can see the original sentence ("Sentença original") to which the highlighted sentence refers.

For the example in Figure 1, the tool presents alternative simplifications containing different subjects, since selecting the correct noun phrase to which an appositive clause was originally linked (which becomes the subject of the new sentence) based on gender and number information was not possible.

At the end of the process, the user returns to the initial screen and can freely continue editing the text or adding new information to it.

5 Text Simplification for education

Text simplification can be used in several applications. Journalists can use it to write simple and straightforward news texts. Government agencies can create more accessible texts to a large number of people. Authors of manuals and technical documents can also benefit from the simplification technology. Simplification techniques can also be used in an educational setting, for example, by a teacher who is creating simplified texts to students. Classic literature books, for example, can be quite hard even to experienced readers. Some genres of texts already have simplified versions, even though the simplification level can be inadequate to a specific target audience. For instance, 3rd and 7th grade students have distinct comprehension levels.

In our approach, the number and type of simplification operations applied to sentences determine its appropriateness to a given literacy level, allowing the creation of multiple versions of the same text, with different levels of complexity, targeting special student needs.

The *Simplifica* editor allows the teacher to adopt any particular texts to be used in the class, for example, the teacher may wish to talk about current news events with his/her students, which would not be available via any repository of simplified texts. The teacher can customize the text generating process and gradually increase the text complexity as his/her students comprehension skills evolve. The use of the editor also helps the teacher to develop a special awareness of the language, which can improve his/her interaction with the students.

Students can also use the system whenever they have difficulties to understand a text given in the classroom. After a student reads the simplified text, the reading of the original text becomes easier, as a result of the comprehension of the simplified text. In this scenario, reading the original text can also help the students to learn new and more complex words and syntactic structures, which would be harder for them without reading of the simplified text.

6 Conclusions

The potentialities of text simplification systems for education are evident. For students, it is a first step for more effective learning. Under another perspective, given the Brazilian population literacy levels, we consider text simplification a necessity. For poor literacy people, we see text simplification as a first step towards social inclusion, facilitating and developing reading and writing skills for people to interact in society. The social impact of text simplification is undeniable.

In terms of language technology, we not only introduced simplification tools in this paper, but also investigated which linguistic phenomena should be simplified and how to simplify them. We also developed a representation schema and designed an on-line authoring system. Although some aspects of the research are language dependent, most of what we propose may be adapted to other languages.

Next steps in this research include practical applications of such technology and the measurement of its impact for both education and social inclusion.

Acknowledgments

We thank the Brazilian Science Foundation FAPESP and Microsoft Research for financial support.

References

Aluísio, S.M., Specia, L., Pardo, T.A.S., Maziero, E.G., Fortes, R. 2008. Towards Brazilian Portuguese Automatic Text Simplification Systems. In the *Proceedings of the 8th ACM Symposium on Document Engineering*, pp. 240-248.

Bick, E. 2000. *The parsing system "Palavras":*

Automatic grammatical analysis of Portuguese in a constraint grammar framework. PhD Thesis University of Århus, Denmark.

Burstein, J. 2009. Opportunities for Natural Language Processing Research in Education. In the *Proceedings of CICLing*, pp. 6-27.

Caseli, H., Pereira, T.F., Specia, L., Pardo, T.A.S., Gasperin, C., Aluisio, S. 2009. Building a Brazilian Portuguese Parallel Corpus of Original and Simplified Texts. In the *Proceedings of CICLing*.

Caseli, H.M.; Nunes, M.G.V.; Forcada, M.L. 2008. Automatic induction of bilingual resources from aligned parallel corpora: application to shallow-transfer machine translation. *Machine Translation*, V. 1, p. 227-245.

Devlin, S., Unthank, G. 2006. Helping aphasic people process online information. In the *Proceedings of the ACM SIGACCESS Conference on Computers and Accessibility*, pp. 225-226.

Graesser, A., McNamara, D. S., Louwerse, M., Cai, Z. 2004. Coh-Metrix: Analysis of text on cohesion and language. *Behavioral Research Methods, Instruments, and Computers*, V. 36, pp. 193-202.

Inui, K., Fujita, A., Takahashi, T., Iida, R., Iwakura, T. 2003. Text Simplification for Reading Assistance: A Project Note. In the *Proceedings of the Second International Workshop on Paraphrasing*, 9 -16.

Klebanov, B., Knight, K., Marcu, D. 2004. Text Simplification for Information-Seeking Applications. *On the Move to Meaningful Internet Systems*. LNCS, V.. 3290, pp. 735-747.

Lal, P., Ruger, S. 2002. Extract-based summarization with simplification. In the *Proceedings of DUC*.

Mapleson, D.L. 2006. *Post-Grammatical Processing for Discourse Segmentation*. PhD Thesis. School of Computing Sciences, University of East Anglia, Norwich.

Max, A. 2005. Simplification interactive pour la production de textes adapt ́es aux personnes souffrant de troubles de la compr ́ehension. In the *Proceedings of Traitement Automatique des Langues Naturelles (TALN)*.

Max, A. 2006. Writing for language-impaired readers. In the *Proceedings of CICLing*, pp. 567-570.

Muniz, M.C., Laporte, E. Nunes, M.G.V. 2005. UNITEX-PB, a set of flexible language resources for Brazilian Portuguese. In *Anais do III Workshop em Tecnologia da Informação e da Linguagem Humana*, V. 1, pp. 1-10.

Pardo, T.A.S. and Nunes, M.G.V. 2008. On the Development and Evaluation of a Brazilian Portuguese Discourse Parser. *Journal of Theoretical and Applied Computing*, V. 15, N. 2, pp. 43-64.

Petersen, S.E. 2007. *Natural Language Processing Tools for Reading Level Assessment and Text Simplification for Bilingual Education*. PhD Thesis, University of Washington.

Petersen, S.E. and Ostendorf, M. 2007. Text Simplification for Language Learners: A Corpus Analysis. In the *Proceedings of the Speech and Language Technology for Education Workshop*, pp. 69-72.

Specia, L., Aluísio, S.M., Pardo, T.A.S. 2008. *Manual de simplificação sintática para o português*. Technical Report NILC-TR-08-06, NILC.

Siddharthan, A. 2002. An Architecture for a Text Simplification System. In the *Proceedings of the Language Engineering Conference*, pp. 64-71.

Siddharthan, A. 2003. *Syntactic Simplification and Text Cohesion*. PhD Thesis. University of Cambridge.

Snow, C. 2002. *Reading for understanding: Toward an R&D program in reading comprehension*. Santa Monica, CA.

An Application of Latent Semantic Analysis to Word Sense Discrimination for Words with Related and Unrelated Meanings

Juan Pino and **Maxine Eskenazi**
(jmpino, max)@cs.cmu.edu
Language Technologies Institute
Carnegie Mellon University
Pittsburgh, PA 15213, USA

Abstract

We present an application of Latent Semantic Analysis to word sense discrimination within a tutor for English vocabulary learning. We attempt to match the meaning of a word in a document with the meaning of the same word in a fill-in-the-blank question. We compare the performance of the Lesk algorithm to Latent Semantic Analysis. We also compare the performance of Latent Semantic Analysis on a set of words with several unrelated meanings and on a set of words having both related and unrelated meanings.

1 Introduction

In this paper, we present an application of Latent Semantic Analysis (LSA) to word sense discrimination (WSD) within a tutor for English vocabulary learning for non-native speakers. This tutor retrieves documents from the Web that contain target words a student needs to learn and that are at an appropriate reading level (Collins-Thompson and Callan, 2005). It presents a document to the student and then follows the document reading with practice questions that measure how the student's knowledge has evolved. It is important that the fill-in-the-blank questions (also known as cloze questions) that we ask to the students allow us to determine their vocabulary knowledge accurately. An example of cloze question is shown in Figure 1.

Some words have more than one meaning and so the cloze question we give could be about a different meaning than the one that the student learned in the document. This is something that can lead to confusion and must be avoided. To do this, we need to use some automatic measure of semantic similarity.

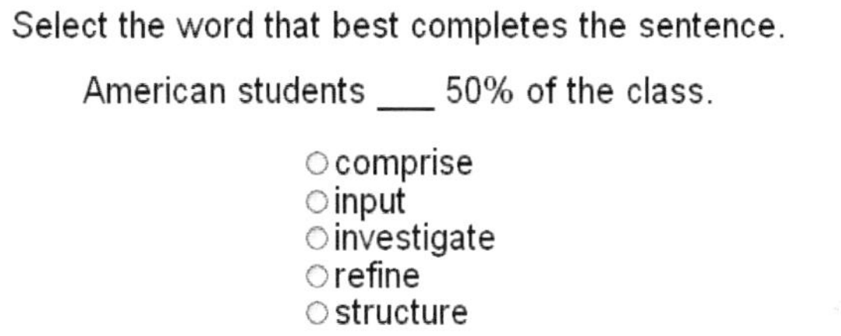

Figure 1: Example of cloze question.

To define the problem formally, given a target word w, a string r (the reading) containing w and n strings q_1, ..., q_n (the sentences used for the questions) each containing w, find the strings q_i where the meaning of w is closest to its meaning in r. We make the problem simpler by selecting only one question.

This problem is challenging because the context defined by cloze questions is short. Furthermore, a word can have only slight variations in meaning that even humans find sometimes difficult to distinguish. LSA was originally applied to Information Retrieval (Dumais et al., 1988). It was shown to be able to match short queries to relevant documents even when there were no exact matches between the words. Therefore LSA would seem to be an appropriate technique for matching a short context, such as a question, with a whole document.

So we are looking to first discriminate between the meanings of words, such as "compound", that have several very different meanings (a chemical compound or a set of buildings) and then to disambiguate words that have senses that are closely related such as "comprise" ("be composed of" or "compose"). In the following sections, we present

Proceedings of the NAACL HLT Workshop on Innovative Use of NLP for Building Educational Applications, pages 43–46,
Boulder, Colorado, June 2009.

LSA and some of its applications, then we present some experimental results that compare a baseline to the use of LSA for both tasks we have just described. We expect the task to be easier on words with unrelated meanings. In addition, we expect that LSA will perform better when we use context selection on the documents.

2 Related Work

LSA was originally applied to Information Retrieval (Dumais et al., 1988) and called Latent Semantic Indexing (LSI). It is based on the singular value decomposition (SVD) theorem. A $m \times n$ matrix X with $m \geq n$ can be written as $X = U \cdot S \cdot V^T$ where U is a $m \times n$ matrix such that $U^T \cdot U = I_m$; S is a $n \times n$ diagonal matrix whose diagonal coefficients are in decreasing order; and V is a $n \times n$ matrix such that $V^T \cdot V = I_n$.

X is typically a term-document matrix that represents the occurrences of vocabulary words in a set of documents. LSI uses truncated SVD, that is it considers the first r columns of U (written U_r), the r highest coefficients in S (S_r) and the first r columns of V (V_r). Similarity between a query and a document represented by vectors $\mathbf{d}$ and $\mathbf{q}$ is performed by computing the cosine similarity between $S_r^{-1} \cdot U_r^T \cdot \mathbf{d}$ and $S_r^{-1} \cdot U_r^T \cdot \mathbf{q}$. The motivation for computing similarity in a different space is to cope with the sparsity of the vectors in the original space. The motivation for truncating SVD is that only the most meaningful semantic components of the document and the query are represented after this transformation and that noise is discarded.

LSA was subsequently applied to number of problems, such as synonym detection (Landauer et al., 1998), document clustering (Song and Park, 2007), vocabulary acquisition simulation (Landauer and Dumais, 1997), etc.

Levin and colleagues (2006) applied LSA to word sense discrimination. They clustered documents containing ambiguous words and for a test instance of a document, they assigned the document to its closest cluster. Our approach is to assign to a document the question that is closest. In addition, we examine the cases where a word has several unrelated meanings and where a word has several closely related meanings.

3 Experimental Setup

We used a database of 62 manually generated cloze questions covering 16 target words[1]. We manually annotated the senses of the target words in these questions using WordNet senses (Fellbaum, 1998). For each word and for each sense, we manually gathered documents from the Web containing the target word with the corresponding sense. There were 84 documents in total. We added 97 documents extracted from the tutor database of documents that contained at least one target word but we did not annotate their meaning.

We wanted to evaluate the performances of LSA for WSD for words with unrelated meanings and for words with both related and unrelated meanings. For the first type of evaluation, we retained four target words. For the second type of evaluation, all 16 words were included. We also wanted to evaluate the influence of the size of the context of the target words. We therefore considered two matrices: a term-document matrix and a term-context matrix where context designates five sentences around the target word in the document. In both cases each cell of the matrix had a *tf-idf* weight. Finally, we wanted to investigate the influence of the dimension reduction on performance. In our experiments, we explored these three directions.

4 Results

4.1 Baseline

We first used a variant of the Lesk algorithm (Lesk, 1986), which is based on word exact match. This algorithm seems well suited for the unsupervised approach we took here since we were dealing with discrimination rather than disambiguation. Given a document $\mathbf{d}$ and a question $\mathbf{q}$, we computed the number of word tokens that were shared between $\mathbf{d}$ and $\mathbf{q}$, excluding the target word. The words were lower cased and stemmed using the Porter stemmer. Stop words and punctuation were discarded; we used the standard English stopword list. Finally, we selected a window of nw words around the target word in the question $\mathbf{q}$ and a window of ns sentences around the target word in the document $\mathbf{d}$. In order to detect sentence boundaries, we used

[1]available at: www.cs.cmu.edu/ jmpino/questions.xls

the OpenNLP toolkit (Baldridge et al., 2002). With $nw = 10$ and $ns = 2$, we obtained an accuracy of 61% for the Lesk algorithm. This can be compared to a random baseline of 44% accuracy.

4.2 LSA

We indexed the document database using the Lemur toolkit (Allan et al., 2003). The database contained both the manually annotated documents and the documents used by the tutor and containing the target words. The Colt package (Binko et al.,) was used to perform singular value decomposition and matrix operations because it supports sparse matrix operations. We explored three directions in our analysis. We investigated how LSA performs for words with related meanings and for words with unrelated meanings. We also explored the influence of the truncation parameter r. Finally, we examined if reducing the document to a selected context of the target word improved performance.

Figures 2 and 3 plot accuracy versus dimension reduction in different cases. In all cases, LSA outperforms the baseline for certain values of the truncation parameter and when context selection was used. This shows that LSA is well suited for measuring semantic similarity between two contexts when at least one of them is short. In general, using the full dimension in SVD hurts the performances. Dimension reduction indeed helps discarding noise and noise is certainly present in our experiments since we do not perform stemming and do not use a stopword list. One could argue that filling the matrix cells with *tf-idf* weights already gives less importance to noisy words.

Figure 2 shows that selecting context in documents does not give much improvement in accuracy. It might be that the amount of context selected depends on each document. Here we had a fixed size context of five sentences around the target word.

In Figure 3, selecting context gives some improvement, although not statistically significant, over the case with the whole document as context. The best performance obtained for words with unrelated meanings and context selection is also better than the performance for words with related and unrelated meanings.

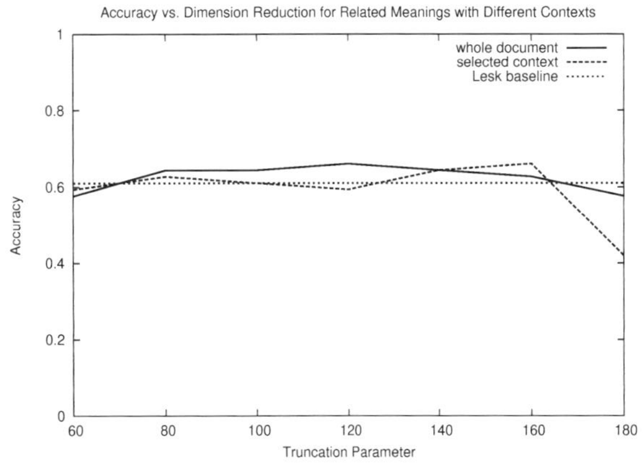

Figure 2: Accuracy vs. r, the truncation parameter, for words with related and unrelated meanings and with whole document or selected context (95% confidence for whole document: [0.59; 0.65], 95% confidence for selected context: [0.52; 0.67])

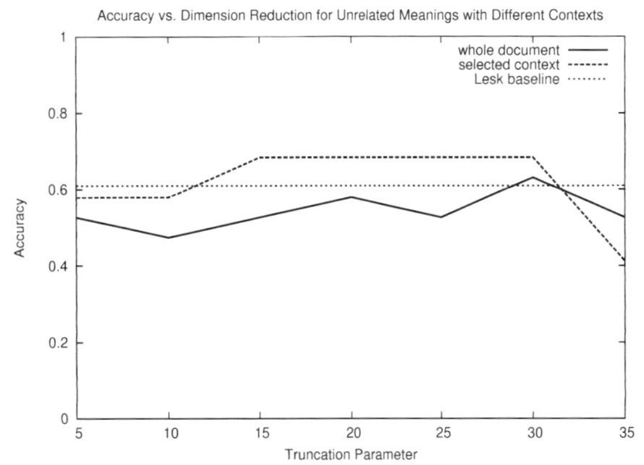

Figure 3: Accuracy vs. r, the truncation parameter, for words with unrelated meanings only and with whole documents or selected context ((95% confidence for whole document: [0.50; 0.59], 95% confidence for selected context: [0.52; 0.71]))

5 Discussion

LSA helps overcome sparsity of short contexts such as questions and gives an improvement over the exact match baseline. However, reducing the context of the documents to five sentences around the target word does not seem to give significant improvement. This might be due to the fact that capturing the right context for a meaning is a difficult task and that a fixed size context does not always represent a relevant context. It is yet unclear how to set the truncation parameter. Although dimension reduction seems to help, better results are sometimes obtained when the truncation parameter is close to full dimension or when the truncation parameter is farther from the full dimension.

6 Conclusion and Future Work

We have shown that LSA, which can be considered as a second-order representation of the documents and question vectors, is better suited than the Lesk algorithm, which is a first-order representation of vectors, for measuring semantic similarity between a short context such as a question and a longer context such as a document. Dimension reduction was shown to play an important role in the performances. However, LSA is relatively difficult to apply to large amounts of data because SVD is computationally intensive when the vocabulary size is not limited. In the context of tutoring systems, LSA could not be applied on the fly, the documents would need to be preprocessed and annotated beforehand.

We would like to further apply this promising technique for WSD. Our tutor is able to provide definitions when a student is reading a document. We currently provide all available definitions. It would be more beneficial to present only the definitions that are relevant to the meaning of the word in the document or at least to order them according to their semantic similarity with the context. We would also like to investigate how the size of the selected context in a document can affect performance. Finally, we would like to compare LSA performance to other second-order vector representations such as vectors induced from co-occurrence statistics.

Acknowledgments

Thanks Mehrbod Sharifi, David Klahr and Ken Koedinger for fruitful discussions. This research is supported by NSF grant SBE-0354420. Any conclusions expressed here are those of the authors.

References

James Allan, Jamie Callan, Kevin Collins-Thompson, Bruce Croft, Fangfang Feng, David Fisher, John Lafferty, Leah Larkey, Thi N. Truong, Paul Ogilvie, et al. 2003. The lemur toolkit for language modeling and information retrieval.

Jason Baldridge, Thomas Morton, and Gann Bierner. 2002. The opennlp maximum entropy package. Technical report, Technical report, SourceForge.

Pavel Binko, Dino Ferrero Merlino, Wolfgang Hoschek, Tony Johnson, Andreas Pfeiffer, et al. Open source libraries for high performance scientific and technical computing in java.

Kevyn Collins-Thompson and Jamie Callan. 2005. Predicting reading difficulty with statistical language models. *Journal of the American Society for Information Science and Technology*, 56(13):1448–1462.

Susane T. Dumais, George W. Furnas, Thomas K. Landauer, Scott Deerwester, and Richard Harshman. 1988. Using latent semantic analysis to improve access to textual information. In *Proceedings of the SIGCHI conference on Human factors in computing systems*, pages 281–285.

Christiane Fellbaum. 1998. *WordNet: An electronic lexical database*. MIT press.

Thomas K. Landauer and Susan T. Dumais. 1997. A solution to plato's problem: The latent semantic analysis theory of acquisition, induction and representation of knowledge. *Psychological review*, 104:211–240.

Thomas K. Landauer, Peter W. Foltz, and Darrell Laham. 1998. An introduction to latent semantic analysis. *Discourse processes*, 25:259–284.

Michael Lesk. 1986. Automatic sense disambiguation using machine readable dictionaries: How to tell a pine cone from an ice cream cone. In *Proceedings of the 5th annual international conference on Systems Documentation*, pages 24–26.

Esther Levin, Mehrbod Sharifi, and Jerry Ball. 2006. Evaluation of utility of lsa for word sense discrimination. In *Proceedings of HLT/NAACL*, pages 77–80.

Wei Song and Soon Cheol Park. 2007. A novel document clustering model based on latent semantic analysis. In *Proceedings of the Third International Conference on Semantics, Knowledge and Grid*, pages 539–542.

Automated Suggestions for Miscollocations

Anne Li-E Liu
Research Centre for English and Applied Linguistics
University of Cambridge
Cambridge, CB3 9DP,
United Kingdom
lel29@cam.ac.uk

David Wible
Graduate Institute of Learning and Instruction
National Central University
Jhongli City, Taoyuan County
32001, Taiwan
wible45@yahoo.com

Nai-Lung Tsao
Graduate Institute of Learning and Instruction
National Central University
Jhongli City, Taoyuan County
32001, Taiwan
beaktsao@gmail.com

Abstract

One of the most common and persistent error types in second language writing is collocation errors, such as *learn knowledge* instead of *gain* or *acquire knowledge*, or *make damage* rather than *cause damage*. In this work-in-progress report, we propose a probabilistic model for suggesting corrections to lexical collocation errors. The probabilistic model incorporates three features: word association strength (MI), semantic similarity (via WordNet) and the notion of shared collocations (or intercollocability). The results suggest that the combination of all three features outperforms any single feature or any combination of two features.

1 Collocation in Language Learning

The importance and difficulty of collocations for second language users has been widely acknowledged and various sources of the difficulty put forth (Granger 1998, Nesselhauf 2004, Howarth 1998, Liu 2002, inter alia). Liu's study of a 4-million-word learner corpus reveals that verb-noun (VN) miscollocations make up the bulk of the lexical collocation errors in learners' essays. Our study focuses, therefore, on VN miscollocation correction.

2 Error Detection and Correction in NLP

Error detection and correction have been two major issues in NLP research in the past decade. Projects involving learner corpora in analyzing and categorizing learner errors include NICT Japanese Learners of English (JLE), the Chinese Learners of English Corpus (Gamon et al., 2008) and English Taiwan Learner Corpus (or TLC) (Wible et al., 2003). Studies that focus on providing automatic correction, however, mainly deal with errors that derive from closed-class words, such as articles (Han et al., 2004) and prepositions (Chodorow et al., 2007). One goal of this work-in-progress is to address the less studied issue of open class lexical errors, specifically lexical collocation errors.

3 The Present Study

We focus on providing correct collocation suggestions for lexical miscollocations. Three features are employed to identify the correct collocation substitute for a miscollocation: word association measurement, semantic similarity between the correction candidate and the misused word to be replaced, and intercollocability (i.e., the concept of shared collocates in collocation clusters proposed by Cowie and Howarth, 1995). NLP research on learner errors includes work on error detection and error correction. While we are working on both, here we report specifically on our work on lexical miscollocation correction.

4 Method

We incorporate both linguistic and computational perspectives in our approach. 84 VN miscollocations from Liu's (2002) study were employed as the training and the testing data in that each comprised 42 randomly chosen miscollocations. Two experienced English teachers[1] manually went through the 84 miscollocations and provided a list of correction suggestions. Only when the system output matches to any of the suggestions offered

[1] One native speaker and one experienced non-native English teacher.

Proceedings of the NAACL HLT Workshop on Innovative Use of NLP for Building Educational Applications, pages 47–50,
Boulder, Colorado, June 2009.

by the two annotators would the data be included in the result. The two main knowledge resources that we incorporated are British National Corpus[2] and WordNet (Miller, 1990). BNC was utilized to measure word association strength and to extract shared collocates while WordNet was used in determining semantic similarity. Our probabilistic model that combines the features is described in sub-section 4.4. Note that all the 84 VN miscollocations are combination of incorrect verbs and focal nouns, our approach is therefore aimed to find the correct verb replacements.

4.1 Word Association Measurement

The role of word association in miscollocation suggestions are twofold: 1. all suggested correct collocations in any case have to be identified as collocations; thus, we assume candidate replacements for the miscollocate verbs must exceed a threshold word association strength with the focal noun; 2. we examine the possibility that the higher the word association score the more likely it is to be a correct substitute for the wrong collocate. We adopt Mutual Information (Church et al. 1991) as our association measurement.

4.2 Semantic Similarity

Both Gitsaki et al. (2000) and Liu (2002) suggest a semantic relation holds between a miscollocate and its correct counterpart. Following this, we assume that in the 84 miscollocations, the miscollocates should stand in more or less a semantic relation with the corrections. For example, *say* in an attested learner miscollocation *say story* is found to be a synonym of the correct verb *tell* in WordNet. Based on this assumption, words that show some degree of semantic similarity with the miscollocate are considered possible candidates for replacing it. To measure similarity we take the synsets of WordNet to be nodes in a graph. We quantify the semantic similarity of the incorrect verb in a miscollocation with other possible substitute verbs by measuring graph-theoretic distance between the synset containing the miscollocate verb and the synset containing candidate substitutes. In cases of polysemy, we take the closest synsets for the distance measure. If the miscollocate and the candidate substitute occur in the same synset, then the distance between them is zero.

The similarity measurement function is as follows (Tsao et al., 2003):

$$sim(w_1, w_2) = \max_{s_i \in synset(w_1), s_j \in synset(w_2)} \left(1 - \frac{dis(s_i, s_j)}{2 \times \max(L_{s_i}, L_{s_j})}\right)$$

,where $dis(s_i, s_j)$ means the node path length between the synset s_i and s_j in WordNet hyper/hypo tree. L_s means the level number of s in hyper/hypo tree and the level of top node is 1. Multiplying $\max(L_{s_i}, L_{s_j})$ by 2 ensures the similarity is less than 1. If s_i and s_j are synonymous, the similarity will be 1.

4.3 Shared Collocates in Collocation Clusters

Futagi et al (2008) review several studies which adopt computational approaches in tackling collocation errors; yet none of them, including Futagi et al., include the notion of collocation cluster. We borrow the cluster idea from Cowie & Howarth (1995) who propose 'overlapping cluster' to denote sets of collocations that carry similar meaning and shared collocates. Figure 1 represents a collocation cluster that expresses the concept of 'bringing something into actuality.' The key here is that not all VN combinations in Figure 1 are acceptable. While *fulfill* and *achieve* collocate with the four nouns on the right, *realize* does not collocate with *purpose,* as indicated by the dotted line. Cowie and Howarth's point is that collocations that can be clustered via overlapping collocates can be the source of collocation errors for language learners. That both *fulfill* and *reach* collocate with *goal* and the further collocability of *fulfill* with *ambition* and *purpose* plausibly lead learners to assume that *reach* shares this collocability as well, leading by overgeneralization to the miscollocations *reach an ambition* or *reach a purpose*.

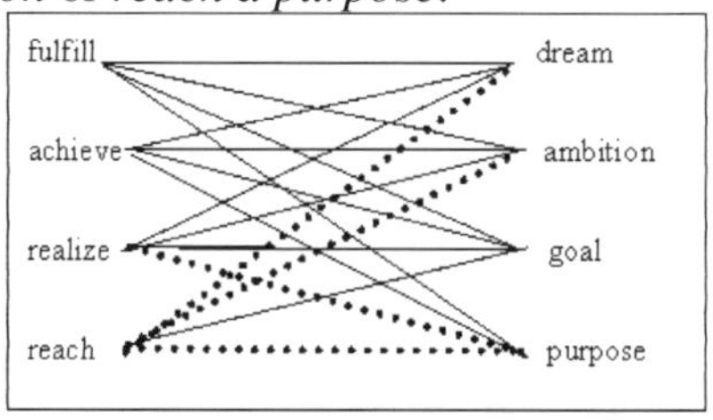

Figure 1. Collocation cluster of 'bringing something into actuality'

[2] *The British National Corpus*, version 3 (BNC XML Edition). 2007. URL: http://www.natcorp.ox.ac.uk/

We employ the ideas of 'collocation cluster' and 'shared collocates' in identifying correct counterparts to the miscollocations. Specifically, taking the miscollocation *reach their purpose* as a starting point, our system generates a collocation cluster by finding the verbs that collocate with *purpose* and nouns that *reach* collocates with. We consider this formed cluster the source that contains the possible correct replacement for *reach* in *reach their purpose*. By finding verbs that not only collocate with *purpose* but also share the most other collocating nouns with the wrong verb *reach*, successfully, we identified candidate substitutes *fulfill* and *achieve* for the incorrect verb *reach*.

4.4 Our Probabilistic Model

The three features we described above are integrated into a probabilistic model. Each feature is used to look up the correct collocation suggestion for a miscollocation. For instance, *cause damage*, one of the possible suggestions for the miscollocation *make damage*, is found to be ranked the 5th correction candidate by using word association measurement merely, the 2nd by semantic similarity and the 14th by using shared collocates. If we combine the three features, however, *cause damage* is ranked first.

The conditional probability of the case where the candidate is a correct one can be presented as:

$$P\ (c\ is\ a\ correct\ verb\ |F_{c,m}\ )$$

where c means a candidate for a specific miscollocation and $F_{c,m}$ means the features values between m (misused words) and c (candidates). According to Bayes theorem and Bayes assumption, which assume that these features are independent, the probability can be computed by:

$$P(S_c|F_{c,m}) = \frac{P(F_{c,m}|\ S_c)\,P(S_c)}{P(F_{c,m})} \approx \frac{\prod_{f\in F_{c,m}} P(f|\ S_c)P(S_c)}{\prod_{f\in F_{c,m}} P(f)}$$

where S_c means the situation 'c is a correct verb', as described above and f is one of the three particular features. We use probability values to choose and rank the K-best suggestions.

5 Experimental Results

Any found VN combination via our probabilistic approach was compared to the suggestions made by the two human experts. A match would be counted as a true positive. A discrete probability distribution is produced for each feature. We divided feature value into five levels and obtained prior predicting value for each level of the three features. For example, we divided MI value to five levels (<1.5, 1.5~3.0, 3.0~4.5, 4.5~6, >6). The five ranks for semantic similarity and normalized shared collocates number are 0.0~0.2, 0.2~0.4, 0.4~0.6, 0.6~0.8 and 0.8 ~1.0. For every feature, we obtain a predicting value for each level after the training process. The predicting value is shown as $\frac{P(f|\ S_c)}{P(f)}$. In line with that, $P(MI>6)$ means the probability of all VN collocations retrieved from BNC in which the MI value is higher than 6 whereas $P(MI>6|\ S_c)$ shows the probability of all correct VN collocations with the MI value higher than 6.

Different combinations of the three features are made on the basis of the probabilistic model described in Section 4.4. Seven models derive from such combinations (See Table 1). Table 2 shows the precision of k-best suggestions for each model.

Models	Feature(s) considered
M 1	MI (Mutual Information)
M 2	SS (Semantic Similarity)
M 3	SC (Shared Collocates)
M 4	MI + SS
M 5	MI + SC
M 6	SS + SC
M 7	MI + SS + SC

Table 1. Models of feature combinations.

K-Best	M1	M2	M3	M4	M5	M6	M7
1	16.67	40.48	22.62	48.81	29.76	55.95	53.57
2	36.90	53.57	38.10	60.71	44.05	63.1	67.86
3	47.62	64.29	50.00	71.43	59.52	77.38	78.57
4	52.38	67.86	63.10	77.38	72.62	80.95	82.14
5	64.29	75.00	72.62	83.33	78.57	83.33	85.71
6	65.48	77.38	75.00	85.71	83.33	84.52	88.10
7	67.86	80.95	77.38	86.90	86.90	86.9	89.29
8	70.24	83.33	82.14	86.90	89.29	88.1	91.67
9	72.62	86.90	85.71	88.10	92.86	90.48	92.86
10	76.19	86.90	88.10	88.10	94.05	90.48	94.05

Table 2. The precision rate of Model 1- 7.

K-Best	M2	M6	M7
1	aim	*obtain	*acquire
2	generate	share	share
3	draw	*develop	*obtain
4	*obtain	generate	*develop
5	*develop	*acquire	*gain

Table 3. The K-Best suggestions for *get knowledge*.

Table 2 shows that, considering the results for each feature run separately (M1-M3), the feature 'semantic similarity' (M2) outperforms the other two. Among combined feature models (M4-M7), M7 (MI + SS+ SC), provides the highest proportion of true positives at every value of k except k = 1. The full hybrid of all three features (M7) outperforms any single feature. The best results are achieved when taking into account both statistical and semantic features. This is illustrated with results for the example *get knowledge* in Table 3 (the asterisks (*) indicate the true positives.)

6 Conclusion

In this report of work in progress, we present a probabilistic model that adopts word association measurement, semantic similarity and shared collocates in looking for corrections for learners' miscollocations. Although only VN miscollocations are examined, the model is designed to be applicable to other types of miscollocations. Applying such mechanisms to other types of miscollocations as well as detecting miscollocations will be the next steps of this research. Further, a larger amount of miscollocations should be included in order to verify our approach and to address the issue of the small drop of the full-hybrid M7 at k=1.

Acknowledgments

The work reported in this paper was partially supported by the grants from the National Science Council, Taiwan (Project Nos. 96-2524-S-008-003- and 98-2511-S-008-002-MY2)

References

Anne. Li-E Liu 2002. *A Corpus-based Lexical Semantic Investigation of VN Miscollocations in Taiwan Learners' English*. Master Thesis, Tamkang University, Taiwan.

Anthony P Cowie and Peter Howarth. 1995. Phraseological Competence and Written Proficiency, Paper Presented at the *British Association of Applied Linguistics Conference* (BAAL), Southampton, England, September.

Christina Gitsaki, Nagoya Shoka Daigaku, and Richard P. Taylor. 2000. English Collocations and Their Place in the EFL Classroom, Available at: http://www.hum.nagoya-cu.ac.jp/~taylor/publications/collocations.html.

Claudia Leacock and Martin Chodorow. 2003. Automated Grammatical Error Detection, In MD Shermis & JC Burstein (Eds.), *Automated Essay Scoring: A Cross-disciplinary*, Mahwah, NJ: Lawrence Erlbaum Associates.

David Wible, Chin-Hwa Kuo, Nai-Lung Tsao, Anne Li-E Liu, and Hsiu-Lin Lin. 2003. Bootstrapping in a Language Learning Environment. *Journal of Computer Assisted Learning*, 19, 90-102.

George Miller. 1990. WordNet: An On-line Lexical Database, *International Journal of Lexicography.*

Kenji Kita and Hiroaki Ogata. 1997. Collocations in Language Learning: Corpus-based Automatic compilation of Collocations and Bilingual Collocation Concordancer, *Computer Assisted Language Learning*. Vol.10, No. 3, 229-238.

Kenneth Church, William Gale, Patrick Hanks and Donald Hindle. 1991. Using Statistics in Lexical Analysis, in Zernik (ed), *Lexical Acquisition: Using On-line Resources to Build a Lexicon, Lawrence Erlbaum*, pp. 115-164.

Martin Chodorow, Joel R. Tetreault and Na-Rae Han. 2007. Detection of Grammatical Errors Involving Prepositions, *Proceedings of the 45th Annual Meeting of the Association for Computational Linguistics, Special Interest Group on Semantics*, Workshop on Prepositions, 25-30.

Michael Gamon, Jianfeng Gao, Chris Brockett, Alexandre Klementiev, William B. Dolan, Dmitriy Belenko, Lucy Vanderwende. 2008. Using Contextual Speller Techniques and Language Modeling for ESL Error Correction, *Proceedings of The Third International Joint Conference on Natural Language Processing,* Hyderabad, India.

Na-Rae Han, Martin Chodorow and Claudia Leacock. 2004. Detecting Errors in English Article Usage with a Maximum Entropy Classifier Trained on a Large, Diverse Corpus, *Proceedings of the 4th International Conference on Language Resources and Evaluation*, Lisbon, Portugal.

Nai-Lung Tsao, David Wible and Chin-Hwa Kuo. 2003. Feature Expansion for Word Sense Disambiguation, *Proceedings of the International Conference on Natural Language Processing and Knowledge Engineering*, 126-131.

Peter Howarth. 1998. Phraseology and Second Language Acquisition. *Applied Linguistics*. 19/1, 24-44.

Yoko Futagi, Paul Deane, Martin Chodorow & Joel Tetreault. 2008. A computational approach to detecting collocation errors in the writing of non-native speakers of English. *Computer Assisted Language Learning*,21:4,353 — 367

A Method for Unsupervised Broad-Coverage Lexical Error Detection and Correction

Nai-Lung Tsao
Graduate Institute of Learning and Instruction
National Central University
Jhongli City, Taoyuan County 32001, Taiwan
beaktsao@gmail.com

David Wible
Graduate Institute of Learning and Instruction
National Central University
Jhongli City, Taoyuan County 32001, Taiwan
Wible45@yahoo.com

Abstract

We describe and motivate an unsupervised lexical error detection and correction algorithm and its application in a tool called Lexbar appearing as a query box on the Web browser toolbar or as a search engine interface. Lexbar accepts as user input candidate strings of English to be checked for acceptability and, where errors are detected, offers corrections. We introduce the notion of hybrid n-gram and extract these from BNC as the knowledgebase against which to compare user input. An extended notion of edit distance is used to identify most likely candidates for correcting detected errors. Results are illustrated with four types of errors.

1 Introduction

We describe and motivate an unsupervised lexical error detection and correction algorithm and its application in a tool called Lexbar appearing as a query box in a web-based corpus search engine or on the Web browser toolbar. The tool is intended as a proxy for search engines in the common practice where users put search engines to use as error checkers. A problem with this use of search engines like Google is that such searches commonly provide false positives, hits for strings that contain errors. Lexbar accepts as user input candidate strings of English to be checked for acceptability and, where errors are detected, offers corrections.

2 Related Work

Among the many works on error detection, recently unsupervised error detection approaches have been proposed, such as [Chodorow and Leacock, 2000] and [Quixal and Badia 2008]. These use contextual features and statistical word association measurement to decide if the detected bigram or trigram is an error or not. To our knowledge, such unsupervised methods have not been applied in error correction. [Gamon et al 2008] and [Felice and Pulman 2008] propose unsupervised approaches to build a probabilistic model for detecting errors (prepositions and articles) and providing correct answers. They also typically focus on a particular type of error, usually limited to a specific word class such as preposition errors, often in a pre-determined paradigmatic slot. Our approach reported here is unsupervised in both detection and correction and is not tailored to a specific target error subtype or targeted to a specific position in a string. More generally the family of error types suitable for this approach are lexical or lexico-grammatical errors since detection and correction are based on patterns of word use detected statistically. At the core of our approach is a bank of what we call "hybrid n-grams" extracted from BNC to serve as the target knowledge against which learner input is compared for detection and correction. We illustrate the single algorithm with results on four different categories of errors.

3 Overview of the Algorithm

The Lexbar application consists of two main components: (1) the target language knowledgebase of hybrid n-grams that serves as the standard against which learner production is examined for errors, and (2) the error detection and correction algorithm that uses this knowledgebase to evalu-

Proceedings of the NAACL HLT Workshop on Innovative Use of NLP for Building Educational Applications, pages 51–54, Boulder, Colorado, June 2009. ©2009 Association for Computational Linguistics

ate learner production through matching and edit distance. Relatively broad coverage is achieved from one algorithm since no specific error type is targeted but violations of word behaviors patterns.

Typically, n-grams are contiguous sequences of lemmas or specific word forms. Using traditional n-grams and string matching against them as a means of error detection leads to weak precision since the absence of a specific n-gram in a standard corpus does not render it an error. To address this limitation, we extend the notion of n-gram to include in the string not only lemmas or word forms but parts-of-speech as well. For example, the chunk *point of view* can be part of a longer string *from my point of view*. Here, the preposition *from* is non-substitutable whereas the possessive pronoun *my* can be replaced by others of the same POS (*his/her/your/*etc.). Hence, replacing the one results in an error (**in my point of view*[1]) while replacing the other is fine (*from her/his/their/our point of view*). The purpose of hybrid n-grams is to introduce the flexibility to capture the appropriate level of abstraction for each slot in a lexical chunk. Hybrid n-grams permit any combination of word forms, lemmas, POSs in a string (see details below). Thus the hybrid n-gram for *from my point of view* is *from [dps] point of view*[2].

For a string of input submitted for error checking, the algorithm first does a matching operation between the input string and the hybrid n-gram bank. The second step for input is finding hybrid n-grams which nearly match the input, using edit distance to measure nearness or similarity. Hybrid n-grams with a distance of 1 or less from the input string are candidates as correction suggestions and are ranked, least distant from the input string ranked as top correction suggestion.

4 The Knowledgebase: Hybrid N-grams

As mentioned in Section 3, a hybrid n-gram bank will be needed. In our model, each slot has four levels of representation to choose from: word form (*enjoys* but not *enjoy or enjoying, etc*); lemma (representing all word forms of that lexeme, e.g., *enjoy, enjoys, and enjoyed, etc*); detailed POS (CLAWS5 with 46 different POSs); rough POS (9 different POSs)[3]. The main challenge is to extract hybrid n-grams which are the optimum combination of representations for each slot to represent a lexical chunk or pattern. One key to this is a pruning method (described below). Clearly, compared with traditional n-gram extraction, the size of our hybrid n-gram bank size will be extremely large if we save all the combinations that can be generated for each n-gram. Considering the example *from my point of view* and setting *point* as the target word, if we only extract hybrid 5-gram strings for it, we will get $2*4^4=512$ (two forms of noun *point* and four forms of others) different hybrid 5-grams. This entails many disadvantages, for example in storage space and processing time. Therefore, we apply several pruning approaches to keep only useful hybrid n-grams in the bank. Another motivation for pruning the bank is to reach optimum recall and precision. The choice of which hybrid n-grams to retain in or discard from the bank directly determines which input strings would be judged as errors and what candidate corrections would be generated for errors. We illustrate the effects of pruning below.

The first criterion for pruning is frequency. Only hybrid n-grams with a frequency greater than the threshold are saved. The second criterion is called **subset pruning**. There will be overlap among different hybrid n-grams. For example, the chunk *from my point of view* could be represented by dozens of hybrid n-grams. Two of them are: (1) *from [dps] point of view*, and (2) *from my point of view*. Notice an input string *from her point of view* would match (1) but not (2). Here the optimum n-gram is (1) because it includes all cases covered by (2) but other acceptable ones as well. Crucially, it is not the case that the more general hybrid n-gram will always yield the more optimum results, however. This must be determined case by case. Consider the first slot in the same chunk *from my point of view*. The following two versions could represent that chunk: (3) *from [dps] point of view* and (4) *[prp] [dps] point of view*[4]. Notice here, however, that it will be the more specific rather than the more inclusive version that is to be preferred. (3) specifies the exact preposition for the chunk whereas (4) would accept any preposition

[1] We use * to represent the error part in n-gram string.

[2] We use [] to represent POS categories. *[dps]* is the CLAWS5 tag for possessive pronoun.

[3] Rough POS includes verb, noun, adj, adv, conj, interj, prep, pron, vm0.

[4] *[prp]* is the CLAWS5 tag for preposition.

(or *[prp]*) occurring in the first slot. But indeed *from* is not freely substitutable in this chunk (cf **in my point of view*). Thus in each slot in each chunk, pruning checks each potential hybrid n-gram against the target corpus to determine statistically the n-grams that capture the optimum degree of substitutability or frozenness for each slot.

This creates an extremely flexible means of representing the knowledgebase. Consider verb complement selection. In examples such as *They enjoy swimming*, the level of generalization is different for the governing verb slot (*enjoy*) on the one hand and the complement (*swimming*) on the other. The right generalization for the complement is a specific verb form but not specific to any one verb. This slot is captured under the CLAWS5 POS *[vvg]* [5], thus permitting *enjoy swimming/reading/sleeping*, but not *enjoy to swim/swam* and so on. Unlike the complement, the governing verb slot here is a specific lexeme (*enjoy swimming* but not *hope swimming; cf hope to swim*) and moreover, it permits that lexeme in any of its word forms (*enjoy/enjoying/enjoyed swimming*). A hybrid n-gram representation has the power to capture these different levels of generalization and restriction in one representation.

Here is how pruning is done. First, we set a **filter factor** ε, where $0<\varepsilon<1$. Assume x and y are two hybrid n-grams and len(x)=len(y). If $x \subset y$ and $|x|/|y| \geq \varepsilon$[6], we will eliminate y from bank. For example, for the two 5-grams *x=from [dps] point of view* and *y=[prp] [dps] point of view*, obviously $x \subset y$ because *from* is a kind of *[prp]* (preposition). If we set the filter factor ε=80% and $|x|/|y|>\varepsilon$, y will be not included in the hybrid n-gram bank. For example from 100M-word BNC, before pruning, there are 110K hybrid n-grams containing target lemma *point*. After pruning, there are only 5K useful hybrid n-grams left.

5 The Edit Distance Algorithm for Error Detection and Correction

5.1 Error Detection

We apply a simple edit distance for error detection by comparing user input n-grams and standard hybrid n-gram in the bank. The approaches are briefly summarized and short examples given in the following:

Step 1: POS tag the user input string and get all hybrid n-grams that can represent that string. For example, a user inputs *in my point of view* and then *[prp] my point of view*, *[prp] [dps] point of view*, *in [dps] point of view*, *in my point of [nn1]*... etc. will be generated. Let C denote the entire set of hybrid n-grams generated from an instance of user input.

Step 2: Search all hybrid n-grams in the target knowledgebase containing *point* or *view*, which are the content words in user input. Let S denote all of the target hybrid n-grams containing *point* or *view*.

Step 3: Compute the edit distance d between every element in C and S. If $\exists d$=0 in (C, S), we assume the user input n-gram is correct. If $\forall d>1$ in (C, S), our system will ignore this case and provide nothing. If $\exists d$=1, we assume the user input might be wrong and the system will enter the error correction procedure.

For efficiency's sake in Step 2, the hybrid n-grams are indexed by content words. We use Levenshtein's edit distance algorithm [Levenshtein 1996] in Step 3. It indicates the difference between user input and standard n-grams in three ways: "substitute relation," i.e., two n-grams are the same length and identical except for one slot. "Delete relation" and "insert relation" hold between two different length n-grams. In this paper we consider only the "substitute relation," such as *in my point of view* and *from my point of view*. This limits edit distance computing to pairs of n-grams of the same length (e.g. 5-gram to 5-gram).

5.2 Error Correction

The system identifies correction candidates from S as those with edit distance d=1 from some member(s) in C. Once the system gets several correction candidates for an input string whose edit distances from user input are 1, we have to decide the ranking of the correct candidates by a value called **weighted edit distance**. Weighted edit distance can identify more appropriate correct n-grams for the user. Imagine a case where an n-gram from C and an n-gram from S show a substitution relation. Assume u is the differing element in the C n-gram and v is its counterpart in the S n-

---

5 *[vvg]* is the CLAWS5 tag for gerund.

6 $|x|$ means the frequency of x in BNC.

gram. Weighted edit distance between these two is computed by the following rules:

Rule 1: If *u* and *v* are both word-forms and are different word-forms of the same lemma (for example *enjoyed* and *enjoying*), given distance α.

Rule 2: If *u* and *v* are both members of CLAWS5 POS and their rough POS are the same, given distance β[7].

Rule 3: If *u* and *v* are both function words, give distance γ.

Rule 4: If *u* and *v* are both content word, give distance δ.

We set α<β and γ<δ. Correct candidate with lower weighted distance makes itself more appropriate for suggestion. For example, before weighting, the error string *pay attention on* gets two distance 1 correct candidates *pay attention to* and *focus attention on*. Weighting will give *pay attention to* a lower weighted distance because *on* and *to* are function words whereas *focus* and *pay* are content words.

6 Experimental Result

Four types of errors shown in Table 1 are examined for our detection and correction algorithm.

Error string	Algorithm result	Correction suggested to user
Preposition		
have a look *of	have a look at	have a look at
I am interested *of	[pnp] **be** interested in	I am interested in
*in my point of view	from [dps] point of view	from my point of view
pay attention *on	pay attention to **pay** attention to	pay attention to
We can discuss *about.	we [vm0] discuss it we [vm0] discuss [noun] we [vm0] discuss [av0]	we can discuss it we can discuss [noun] we can discuss {adv}
Adjectival participles		
He is *confusing with	[pnp] **be** confused [prp]	He is confused with
I am *interesting in	[pnp] **be** interested in	I am interested in
I am *exciting about	[pnp] **be** excited [prp]	I am excited about
Verb form		
He wants *reading.	he wants [vvt] he **want** [vvt]	He wants to read
I enjoy *to read.	i enjoy [vvg] i **enjoy** [vvg]	I enjoy reading
let them *to stay.	let them [vvi] **let** them [vvi]	let them stay
make him *to leave	make him [vvi] **make** him [vvi]	make him leave
must let them *to stay	[vm0] let them [vvi]	must let them stay
spend time to understand	**spend** time [vvg]	spend time understanding
will make him *to leave	will make [pnp] [vvi]	will make him leave
Missing be		
I* afraid of	**be** afraid of [adv] afraid of [av0] afraid of	be afraid of [adv]afraid of [adj] afraid of
They* aware of	**be** aware of [av0] aware of	be aware of [adv]aware of

Table 1: Four error types and their examples with correct suggestions.

7 Conclusion

We propose an algorithm for unsupervised lexical error detection and correction and apply it to a user tool called Lexbar. This is a work-in-progress report, and we have not yet run full testing with a large data set, such as a learner corpus. However the early stage experimental results show promise, especially its broad coverage over different error types compared to error-specific approaches.

Acknowledgments

The work described in this paper was partially supported by the grants from the National Science Council, Taiwan (Project Nos. 96-2524-S-008-003- and 98-2511-S-008-002-MY2)

Reference

Martin Chodorow and Claudia Leacock 2000. An unsupervised method for detecting grammatical errors. *Proceedings of the 1st conference of NAACL*, pages 140–147.

Rachele De Felice and Stephen G. Pulman 2008. Automatic detection of preposition errors in learner writing. *CALICO AALL Workshop*.

M. Gamon, J. Gao, C. Brockett, A. Klementiev, W. B. Dolan, D. Belenko, and L. Vanderwende 2008. Using Contextual Speller Techniques and Language Modeling for ESL Error Correction. *Proceedings of IJCNLP*.

V. I. Levenshtein 1966. Binary codes capable of correcting deletions, insertions, and reversals. *Soviet Physics Doklady*, 10:707–710.

Martí Quixal and Toni Badia 2008. Exploiting unsupervised techniques to predict EFL learner errors. *CALICO AALL Workshop*.

[7] Recall we use two levels of POS tagging in our hybrid n-grams: 1. The detailed one is CLAWS5 with 46 tags. 2. The rough or simple tag set of 9 tags.

KSC-PaL: A Peer Learning Agent that Encourages Students to take the Initiative*

Cynthia Kersey and Barbara Di Eugenio
Department of Computer Science
University of Illinois at Chicago
Chicago, IL 60607 USA
ckerse2@uic.edu
bdieugen@cs.uic.edu

Pamela Jordan and Sandra Katz
Learning Research and Development Center
University of Pittsburgh
Pittsburgh, PA 15260 USA
pjordan+@pitt.edu
katz+@pitt.edu

Abstract

We present an innovative application of discourse processing concepts to educational technology. In our corpus analysis of peer learning dialogues, we found that initiative and initiative shifts are indicative of learning, and of learning-conducive episodes. We are incorporating this finding in KSC-PaL, the peer learning agent we have been developing. KSC-PaL will promote learning by encouraging shifts in task initiative.

1 Introduction

Collaboration in dialogue has long been researched in computational linguistics (Chu-Carroll and Carberry, 1998; Constantino-González and Suthers, 2000; Jordan and Di Eugenio, 1997; Lochbaum and Sidner, 1990; Soller, 2004; Vizcaíno, 2005), however, the study of peer learning from a computational perspective is still in the early stages. This is an important area of study because peer learning has been shown to be an effective mode of learning, potentially for all of the participants (Cohen et al., 1982; Brown and Palincsar, 1989; Birtz et al., 1989; Rekrut, 1992). Additionally, while there has been a focus on using natural language for intelligent tutoring systems (Evens et al., 1997; Graesser et al., 2004; VanLehn et al., 2002), peer to peer interactions are notably different from those of expert-novice pairings, especially with respect to the richness of the problem-solving deliberations and negotiations. Using natural language in collaborative learning could have a profound impact on the way in which educational applications engage students in learning.

Previous research has suggested several mechanisms that explain why peer learning is effective for all participants. Among them are: self-directed explaining(Chi et al., 1994), other-directed explaining (Ploetzner et al., 1999; Roscoe and Chi, 2007) and Knowledge Co-construction – KCC for short (Hausmann et al., 2004). KCC episodes are defined as portions of the dialogue in which students are jointly constructing a shared meaning of a concept required for problem solving. This last mechanism is the most interesting from a peer learning perspective because it is a truly collaborative construct and also because it is consistent with the widely accepted constructivist view of learning.

Since KCC is a high-level concept that is not easily recognized by an artificial agent we collected peer learning interactions from students and studied them to identify features that might be useful in identifying KCC. We found that linguistically based initiative shifts seem to capture the notion of collaborative construction. A more thorough analysis found a strong relationship between KCC and initiative shifts and moderate correlations between initiative shifts and learning.

The results of this analysis are being incorporated into KSC-PaL, an artificial agent that can collaborate with a human student via natural-language dialogue and actions within a graphical workspace. KSC-PaL has been developed in the last two years. Dialogue-wise, its core is TuTalk (Jordan et al., 2007), a dialogue management system that supports natural lan-

*This work is funded by NSF grants 0536968 and 0536959.

Proceedings of the NAACL HLT Workshop on Innovative Use of NLP for Building Educational Applications, pages 55–63,
Boulder, Colorado, June 2009.

guage dialogue in educational applications. As we will describe, we have already developed its user interface and its student model and have extended TuTalk's planner to provide KSC-PaL with the ability to induce initiative shifts. For the version of KSCPal we will present in this paper, we wanted to focus on the question of whether this style of interaction helps learning; and we were concerned that its limitations in disambiguating the student's input could impact this interaction. Hence, this round of experiments employs a human "helper" that is given a list of concepts the input may match, and chooses the most appropriate one.

The work presented in this paper is part of a larger research program: we analyze different paradigms – tutoring dialogues and peer-learning dialogues– in the same basic domain, devise computational models for both, and implement them in two separate SW systems, an ITS and the peer-learning system we present here. For our work on the tutoring dialogue corpus and the ITS please see (Fossati et al., accepted for publication 2009).

Our domain in both cases is problem solving in basic data structure and algorithms, which is part of foundations of Computer Science. While in recent years, interest in CS in the US has dropped dramatically, CS is of enormous strategic interest, and is projected to foster vast job growth in the next few years (AA. VV., 2006). We believe that by supporting CS education in its core we can have the largest impact on reversing the trend of students' disinterest. Our belief is grounded in the observation that the rate of attrition is highest at the earliest phases of undergraduate CS curricula. This is due in part to students' difficulty with mastering basic concepts (Katz et al., 2003), which require a deep understanding of static structures and the dynamic procedures used to manipulate them (AA. VV., 2001). These concepts also require the ability to move seamlessly among multiple representations, such as text, pictures, pseudo-code, and real code in a specific programming language.

Surprisingly, few educational SW systems address CS topics, e.g. teaching a specific programming language like LISP (Corbett and Anderson, 1990) or database concepts (Mitrović et al., 2004). Additionally, basically they are all ITSs, where the relationship between the system and the student is one of "subordination". Only two or three of these ITSs address foundations, including: Autotutor (Graesser et al., 2004) addresses basic literacy, but not data structures or algorithms; ADIS (Warendorf and Tan, 1997) tutors on basic data structures, but its emphasis is on visualization, and it appears to have been more of a proof of concept than a working system; ProPL (Lane and VanLehn, 2003) helps novices design their programs, by stressing problem solving and design skills.

In this paper, we will first discuss the collection and analysis of peer learning interactions. Then, we discuss the design of our peer agent, and how it is guided by the results of our analysis. We conclude by briefly describing the user experiments we are about to undertake, and whose preliminary results will be available at the time of the workshop.

2 Data collection

We have collected peer learning interactions from 15 pairs of students solving problems in the domain of computer science data structures. Students were recruited from introductory courses on data structures and algorithms. Each problem involved one of three types of data structures: linked-lists, stacks and binary search trees. Each problem was either a debugging problem where the students were asked to work together to identify errors in the code or an explanation problems in which the students jointly created an explanation of a segment of code.

The students interacted using a computer mediated interface[1] where they could communicate via text-based chat, drawing and making changes to code (see Figure 1). The graphical workspace (drawing and coding areas) was shared such that changes made by one student were propagated to his/her partner's workspace. Access to this graphical workspace was controlled so that only one student was allowed to draw or make changes to code at any point in time.

Each pair was presented with a total of 5 problems, although not all pairs completed all problems due to time limitations. The interactions for each pair were subdivided into separate dialogues

[1]Using text to communicate versus face-to-face interactions should be comfortable for most students given the prevalence of communication methods such as text messaging and instant messengers.

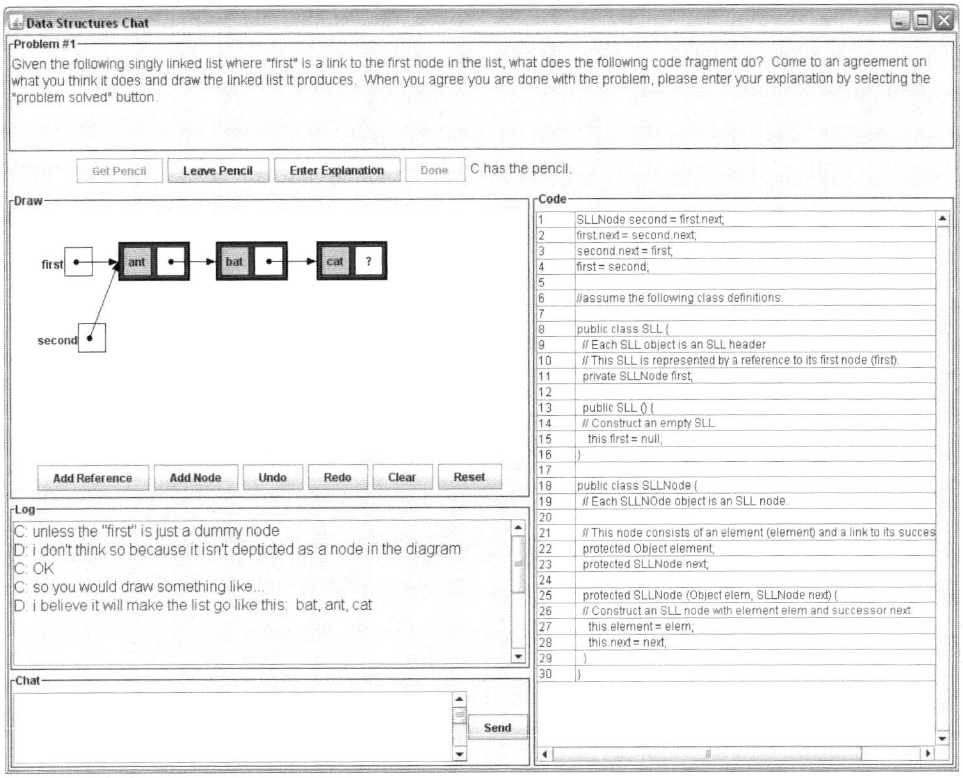

Figure 1: The data collection / KSC-PaL interface

for each problem. Thus, we collected a corpus consisting of a total of 73 dialogues.

In addition to collecting problem solving data, we also presented each student with a pre-test prior to problem solving and an identical post-test at the conclusion of problem solving in order to measure learning gains. A paired t-test of pre- and post-test scores showed that students did learn during collaborative problem solving ($t(30)=2.83$; $p=0.007$). The interactions produced an average normalized learning gain of 17.5 (possible total points are 50).

3 Analysis of Peer Learning Interactions

Next, we undertook an extensive analysis of the corpus of peer learning interactions in order to determine the behaviors with which to endow KSC-PaL.

3.1 Initiative: Annotation

Given the definition of KCC, it appeared to us that the concept of initiative from discourse and dialogue processing should play a role: intuitively, if the students are jointly contructing a concept, the initiative cannot reside only with one, otherwise the partner would just be passive. Hence, we annotated the dialogues for both KCC and initiative.

The KCC annotation involved coding the dialogues for KCC episodes. These are defined as a series of utterances and graphical actions in which students are jointly constructing a shared meaning of a concept required for problem solving (Hausmann et al., 2004). Using this definition, an outside annotator and one of the authors coded 30 dialogues (approximately 46% of the corpus) for KCC episodes. This entailed marking the beginning utterance and the end utterance of such episodes, under the assumption that all intervening utterances do belong to the same KCC episode (otherwise the coder would mark an earlier end for the episode). The resulting intercoder reliability, measured with the Kappa statistic(Carletta, 1996), is considered excellent ($\kappa = 0.80$).

Our annotation of initiative was two fold. Since there is disagreement in the computational linguistics community as to the precise definition of initiative(Chu-Carroll and Carberry, 1998; Jordan and Di Eugenio, 1997), we annotated the dialogues for both dialogue initiative, which tracks who is leading the conversation and determining the current conversational focus, and task initiative, which tracks the lead in problem solving.

For dialogue initiative annotation, we used the well-known utterance-based rules for allocation of control from (Walker and Whittaker, 1990). In this scheme, each utterance is tagged with one of four dialogue acts (assertion, command, question or prompt) and control is then allocated based on a set of rules. The dialogue act annotation was done automatically, by marking turns that end in a question mark as questions, those that start with a verb as commands, prompts from a list of commonly used prompts (e.g. ok, yeah) and the remaining turns as assertions. To verify that the automatic annotation was good, we manually annotated a sizable portion of the dialogues with those four dialogue acts. We then compared the automatic annotation against the human gold standard, and we found an excellent accuracy: it ranged from 86% for assertions and questions, to 97% for prompts, to 100% for commands.

Once the dialogue acts had been automatically annotated, two coders, one of the authors and an outside annotator, coded 24 dialogues (1449 utterances, approximately 45% of the corpus) for dialogue initiative, by using the four control rules from (Walker and Whittaker, 1990):

1. Assertion: Control is allocated to the speaker unless it is a response to a question.
2. Command: Control is allocated to the speaker.
3. Question: Control is allocated to the speaker, unless it is a response to a question or a command.
4. Prompt: Control is allocated to the hearer.

The resulting intercoder reliability on dialogue initiative was 0.77, a quite acceptable level of agreement. We then experimented with automatically annotating dialogue initiative according to those control rules. Since the accuracy against the gold standard was 82%, the remaining 55% of the corpus was also automatically annotated for dialogue initiative, using those four control rules.

As concerns task initiative, we define it as *any action by a participant to either achieve a goal directly, decompose a goal or reformulate a goal* (Guinn, 1998; Chu-Carroll and Brown, 1998). Actions in our domain that show task initiative include:

- Explaining what a section of code does.
- Identifying that a section of code as correct or incorrect.
- Suggesting a correction to a section of code
- Making a correction to a section of code prior to discussion with the other participant.

The same two coders annotated for task initiative the same portion of the corpus already annotated for dialogue initiative. The resulting intercoder reliability for task initiative is 0.68, which is high enough to support tentative conclusions. The outside coder then manually coded the remaining 55% of the corpus for task initiative.

3.2 KCC, initiative and learning

In analyzing the annotated dialogues, we used multiple linear regression to identify correlations of the annotated features and post-test score. We used pre-test score as a covariate because of its significant positive correlations with post-test score. Due to variations in student ability in the different problem types, our analysis focused only on a portion of the collected interactions. In the tree problem there was a wide variation in experience level of the students which would inhibit KCC. In the stack problem, the students had a better understanding of stacks prior to problem solving and spent less time in discussion and problem solving. Thus, our analysis focused only on the linked-list problems.

We started by analyzing the relationship between KCC and learning. As a measurement of KCC we used *KCC actions* which is the number of utterances and graphical actions that occur during KCC episodes. This analysis showed that KCC does have a positive correlation with learning in our corpus. In Table 1, the first row shows the benefit for the dyad overall by correlating the mean post-test score with the mean pre-test score and the dyad's KCC actions. The second row shows the benefit for individuals by correlating individual post-test scores with individual pre-test scores and the dyad's KCC actions. The difference in the strength of these correlations suggests that members of the dyads are not benefitting equally from KCC. If the subjects are divided into two groups, those with a pre-test score below the mean score (n=14) and those with a pre-test score above the mean score (n=16) , it can be seen that those with a low pre-test score benefit more from the KCC episodes than do those with a high pre-test score (rows 3 and 4 in Table 1).

KCC actions predict	β	R^2	p
Mean post-test score	0.43	0.14	0.02
Individual post-test score	0.33	0.08	0.03
Individual post-test score (low pre-test subjects)	0.61	0.37	0.03
Individual post-test score (high pre-test subjects)	0.33	0.09	ns

Table 1: KCC Actions as Predictor of Post-test Score

Next, we explored the relationship between learning and the number of times initiative shifted between the students. Intuitively, we assumed that frequent shifts of initiative would reflect students working together to solve the problem. We found there was a significant correlation between post-test score (after removing the effects of pre-test scores) and the number of shifts in dialogue initiative and the number of shifts in task initiative (see Table 2). This analysis excluded two dyads whose problem solving collaboration had gone awry.

Predictor of Post-test	β	R^2	p
Dialogue initiative shifts	0.45	0.20	0.00
Task initiative shifts	0.42	0.20	0.01

Table 2: Initiative Predictors of Post-test Score

We then computed a second measure of KCC that is meant to reflect the density of the KCC episodes. *KCC initiative shifts* is the number of task initiative shifts that occur during KCC episodes. Many task initiative shifts reflect more active KCC.

Table 3 uses KCC initiative shifts as the measure of co-construction. It shows similar results to table 1, where KCC actions was used. Note that when the outlier dyads were removed the correlation with learning is much stronger for the low pre-test score subjects when KCC initiative shifts are used as the measure of KCC ($R^2 = 0.45, p = 0.02$) than when KCC actions are used.

KCC initiative shifts predict	β	R^2	p
Mean post-test score	0.46	0.15	0.01
Individual post-test score	0.35	0.09	0.02
Individual post-test score (low pre-test subjects)	0.67	0.45	0.02
Individual post-test score (high pre-test subjects)	0.10	0.01	ns

Table 3: KCC Initiative Shifts Predictors of Post-test Score

Lastly we investigated the hypothesis that KCC episodes involve frequent shifts in initiative, as both participants are actively participating in problem solving. To test this hypothesis, we calculated the average initiative shifts per line during KCC episodes and the average initiative shifts per line during problem solving outside of KCC episodes for each dyad. A paired t-test was then used to verify that there is a difference between the two groups. The t-test showed no significant difference in average dialogue initiative shifts in KCC episodes compared with non-KCC problem solving. However, there is a significant difference between average task initiative shifts in KCC episodes compared with the rest of the dialogue (t(57) = 3.32, p = 0.0016). The effect difference between the two groups (effect size = 0.65) shows that there is a meaningful increase in the number of task initiative shifts in KCC episodes compared with problem solving activity outside of the KCC episodes.

3.3 Indicators of task initiative shifts

Since our results show that task initiative shifts are conducive to learning, we want to endow our software agent with the ability to encourage a shift in initiative from the agent to the student, when the student is overly passive. The question is, what are natural indicators in dialogue that the partner should take the initiative? We explored two different methods for encouraging initiative shifts. One is that student uncertainty may lead to a shift in initiative. The other consists of cues for initiative shifts identified in related literature(Chu-Carroll and Brown, 1998; Walker and Whittaker, 1990).

Intuitively, uncertainty by a peer might lead to his partner taking the initiative. One possible identifier of student uncertainty is hedging. To validate this hypothesis, we annotated utterances in the corpus with hedging categories as identified in (Bhatt et al., 2004). Using these categories we were unable to reliably annotate for hedging. But, after collapsing the categories into a single binary value of hedging/not hedging we arrived at an acceptable agreement ($\kappa = 0.71$).

Another identifier of uncertainty is a student's request for feedback from his partner. When uncertain of his contribution, a student may request an evaluation from his peer. So, we annotated utterances with "request for feedback" and were able to arrive at an excellent level of intercoder reliability ($\kappa = 0.82$).

(Chu-Carroll and Brown, 1998) identifies cues that may contribute to the shift of task and dialogue initiative. Since task initiative shifts appear to identify KCC episodes, we chose to explore the following cues that potentially result in the shift of task initiative.

- Give up task. These are utterances where the student explicitly gives up the task using phrases like "Any other ideas?".
- Pause. A pause may suggest that the speaker has nothing more to say in the current turn and intends to give up his initiative.
- Prompts. A prompt is an utterance that has no propositional content.
- Invalid statements. These are incorrect statements made by a student.

Using hedging, request for feedback and initiative cues, we were able to identify 283 shifts in task initiative or approximately 67% of all task initiative shifts in the corpus. The remaining shifts were likely an explicit take over of initiative without a preceding predictor.

Since we found several possible ways to predict and encourage initiative shifts, the next step was to identify which of these predictors more often resulted in an initiative shift; and, for which predictors the resulting initiative shift more often led to an increase in the student's knowledge level. Table 4 shows the percentage of instances of each predictor that resulted in an initiative shift.

Cue/Identifier	Percent of instances that led to initiative shift
Hedge	23.94%
Request feedback	21.88%
Give-up task	20.00%
Pause	25.27%
Prompt	29.29%
Invalid statement	38.64%

Table 4: Cues for Shifts in Initiative

Along with the likelihood of a predictor leading to an initiative shift, we also examined the impact of a shift of task initiative on a student's level of knowledge, measured using knowledge score, calculated on the basis of the student model (see Section 4). This is an important characteristic since we want to encourage initiative shifts in an effort to increase learning. First, we analyzed initiative shifts to determine if they resulted in an increase in knowledge score. We found that in our corpus, an initiative shift leads to an increase in a student's knowledge level in 37.0% of task initiative shifts, a decrease in knowledge level in 5.2% of shifts and unchanged in 57.8% of shifts. Even though over one-half of the time knowledge scores were not impacted, in only a small minority of instances did a shift have a negative impact on a student's level of knowledge. Therefore, we more closely examined the predictors to see which more frequently led to an increase in student knowledge. The results of that analysis is show in table 5.

Predictor	Percent of shifts where knowledge level increased
Hedge	23.52%
Request feedback	17.65%
Give-up task	0.00%
Prompt	32.93%
Pause	14.22%
Invalid statement	23.53%

Table 5: Task Initiative Shifts/Knowledge Level Change

4 KSC-PaL, a software peer

Our peer-learning agent, KSC-PaL, has at its core the TuTalk System(Jordan et al., 2007), a dialogue management system that supports natural language dialogue in educational applications. Since TuTalk does not include an interface or a student model, we developed both in previous years. We also needed to extend the TuTalk planner to recognize and promote initiative shifts.

The user interface is structured similarly to the one used in data collection(see Figure 1). However, we added additional features to allow a student to effectively communicate with the KSC-PaL. First, all drawing and coding actions of the student are interpreted and passed to the agent as a natural language utterance. Graphical actions are matched to a set of known actions and when a student signals that he/she has finished drawing or coding either by ceding control of the graphical workspace or by starting to communicate through typed text, the interface will attempt to match what the student has drawn or coded with its database of known graphical actions. These graphical actions include not only correct ones but also anticipated misconceptions that were collected from the data collection interactions. The second enhancement to the interface is a spell corrector for "chat slang". We found in the corpus, that students often used abbreviations that are common to text messaging. These abbreviations are not recognized by the English language spell corrector in the TuTalk system, so a chat slang interpretation module was added.

KSC-PaL requires a student model to track the current state of problem solving as well as estimate the student's knowledge of concepts involved in solving the problem in order to guide its behavior. Our student model incorporates problem solution graphs (Conati et al., 2002). Solution graphs are Bayesian networks where each node represents either an action required to solve the problem, a concept required as part of problem solving or an anticipated misconception. A user's utterances and actions are then matched to these nodes. A knowledge score can be calculated at any point in time by taking a sum of the probabilities of all nodes in the graph, except the misconception nodes. The sum of the probabilities of the misconception nodes are subtracted from the total to arrive at a knowledge score. This score is then normalized by dividing it by the maximum possible knowledge score for the solution graph.

4.1 KSC-PaL and initiative

Since our corpus study showed that the level of task initiative can be used to identify when KCC and potentially learning is occurring, we have endowed KSC-PaL with behaviors to manipulate shifts in task initiative in order to encourage KCC and learning. This required three enhancements: first, the ability to recognize the initiative holder in each utterance or action; second, the ability to encourage the shift of initiative from the agent to the student; and three, extending the TuTalk planner so that it can process task initiative shifts.

As concerns the first step, that the agent recognize the initiative holder in each utterance or action, we resorted to machine learning. Using the Weka Toolkit(Witten and Frank, 2005), we explored various machine learning algorithms and feature sets that could reliably identify the holder of task initiative. We found that the relevant features of an action in the graphical workspace were substantially different from those of a natural language utterance. Therefore, we trained and tested separate classifiers for each type of student action. After examining a wide variety of machine learning algorithms we selected the following two classifiers: (1) K* (Cleary and Trigg, 1995), a clustering algorithm, for classifying natural language utterances which correctly classified 71.7699% of utterance and (2) JRip (Cohen, 1995), a rule-based algorithm, for classifying drawing and coding actions which correctly classified 86.971% of the instances.

As concerns the second step, encouraging initiative shifts so that the student assumes the task initiative, we use the results of our analysis of the indicators of task initiative shifts from Section 3.3. KSC-PaL will use prompts, request feedback and make invalid statements in order to encourage initiative shifts and promote learning.

Finally, we augmented the TuTalk planner so that it selects scripts to manage task initiative shifts. Two factors will determine whether a script that encourages initiative shifts will be selected: the current level of initiative shifts and the change in the student's knowledge score. Task initiative shifts will be tracked using the classifier described above. Scripts will be selected to encourage initiative shifts when the average level of initiative shifts is less than the mean initiative shifts in KCC episodes (calculated from the corpus data) and the student's knowledge level has not increased since the last time a script selection was requested. The scripts are based on the analysis of methods for encouraging initiative shifts described above. Specifically, KSC-PaL will encourage initiative shifts by responding to student input using prompts, requesting feedback from the student and encouraging student criticism by intentionally making errors in problem solving.

We are now poised to run user experiments. We will run subjects in two conditions with KSC-PaL: in the first condition (control), KSC-PaL will not encourage task initiative shifts and act more as a tutor; in the second condition, KSC-PaL will encourage task initiative shifts as we just discussed. One final note: because we do not want our experiments to be affected by the inability of the agent to interpret an utterance, given current NLU technology, the interface will "incorporate" a human interpreter. The interpreter will receive student utterances along with a list of possible matching concepts from TuTalk. The interpreter will select the most likely matching concept, thus assisting TuTalk in natural language interpretation. Note that the interpreter has a limited, predetermined sets of choices, corresponding to the concepts TuTalk knows about. In this way, his / her intervention is circumscribed.

5 Conclusions

After an extensive analysis of peer-learning interactions, we have found that task initiative shifts can be used to determine when students are engaged in knowledge co-construction. We have embedded this finding in a peer-learning agent, KSC-PaL, that varies its behavior to encourage initiative shifts and knowledge co-construction in order to promote learning. We are poised to run our user experiments, and we will have preliminary results available by the workshop time.

References

AA. VV. 2001. Computer Science, Final Report, The Joint Task Force on Computing Curricula. *IEEE Computer Society and Association for Computing Machinery, IEEE Computer Society.*

AA. VV. 2006. US bureau of labor statistics http://www.bls.gov/oco/oco20016.htm.

Khelan Bhatt, Martha Evens, and Shlomo Argamon. 2004. Hedged responses and expressions of affect in human/human and human computer tutorial interactions. In *Proceedings Cognitive Science*.

M. W. Birtz, J. Dixon, and T. F. McLaughlin. 1989. The effects of peer tutoring on mathematics performance: A recent review. *B. C. Journal of Special Education*, 13(1):17–33.

A. L. Brown and A. S. Palincsar, 1989. *Guided, cooperative learning and individual knowledge acquisition*, pages 307–226. Lawrence Erlbaum Associates, Hillsdale, NJ.

Jean Carletta. 1996. Assessing agreement on classification tasks: the kappa statistic. *Comput. Linguist.*, 22(2):249–254.

M.T.H. Chi, N. De Leeuw, M.H. Chiu, and C. LaVancher. 1994. Eliciting self-explanations improves understanding. *Cognitive Science*, 18(3):439–477.

Jennifer Chu-Carroll and Michael K. Brown. 1998. An evidential model for tracking initiative in collaborative dialogue interactions. *User Modeling and User-Adapted Interaction*, 8(3–4):215–253, September.

Jennifer Chu-Carroll and Sandra Carberry. 1998. Collaborative response generation in planning dialogues. *Computational Linguistics*, 24(3):355–400.

John G. Cleary and Leonard E. Trigg. 1995. K*: An instance-based learner using an entropic distance measure. In *Proc. of the 12th International Conference on Machine Learning*, pages 108–114.

P.A. Cohen, J.A. Kulik, and C.C. Kulik. 1982. Education outcomes of tutoring: A meta-analysis of findings. *American Education Research Journal*, 19(2):237–248.

William W. Cohen. 1995. Fast effective rule induction. In *Machine Learning: Proceedings of the Twelve International Conference*.

Cristina Conati, Abigail Gertner, and Kurt Vanlehn. 2002. Using bayesian networks to manage uncertainty in student modeling. *User Modeling and User-Adapted Interaction*, 12(4):371–417.

María de los Angeles Constantino-González and Daniel D. Suthers. 2000. A coached collaborative learning environment for entity-relationship modeling. *Intelligent Tutoring Systems*, pages 324–333.

Albert T. Corbett and John R. Anderson. 1990. The effect of feedback control on learning to program with the LISP tutor. In *Proceedings of the Twelfth Annual Conference of the Cognitive Science Society*, pages 796–803.

Martha W. Evens, Ru-Charn Chang, Yoon Hee Lee, Leem Seop Shim, Chong Woo Woo, Yuemei Zhang, Joel A. Michael, and Allen A. Rovick. 1997. Circsim-tutor: an intelligent tutoring system using natural language dialogue. In *Proceedings of the fifth conference on Applied natural language processing*, pages 13–14, San Francisco, CA, USA. Morgan Kaufmann Publishers Inc.

Davide Fossati, Barbara Di Eugenio, Christopher Brown, Stellan Ohlsson, David Cosejo, and Lin Chen. accepted for publication, 2009. Supporting Computer Science curriculum: Exploring and learning linked lists with iList. *EEE Transactions on Learning Technologies, Special Issue on Real-World Applications of Intelligent Tutoring Systems*.

Arthur C. Graesser, Shulan Lu, George Tanner Jackson, Heather Hite Mitchell, Mathew Ventura, Andrew Olney, and Max M. Louwerse. 2004. Autotutor: A tutor with dialogue in natural language. *Behavior Research Methods, Instruments, & Computers*, 36:180–192(13), May.

Curry I. Guinn. 1998. An analysis of initiative selection in collaborative task-oriented discourse. *User Modeling and User-Adapted Interaction*, 8(3-4):255–314.

Robert G.M. Hausmann, Michelene T.H. Chi, and Marguerite Roy. 2004. Learning from collaborative problem solving: An analysis of three hypothesized mechanisms. In K.D Forbus, D. Gentner, and T. Regier, editors, *26th Annual Conference of the Cognitive Science Society*, pages 547–552, Mahwah, NJ.

Pamela W. Jordan and Barbara Di Eugenio. 1997. Control and initiative in collaborative problem solving dialogues. In *Working Notes of the AAAI Spring Symposium on Computational Models for Mixed Initiative*, pages 81–84, Menlo Park, CA.

Pamela W Jordan, Brian Hall, Michael A. Ringenberg, Yui Cue, and Carolyn Penstein Rosé. 2007. Tools for authoring a dialogue agent that participates in learning studies. In *Artificial Intelligence in Education, AIED 2007*, pages 43–50.

S. Katz, J. Aronis, D. Allbritton, C. Wilson, and M.L. Soffa. 2003. Gender and race in predicting achievement in computer science. *Technology and Society Magazine, IEEE*, 22(3):20–27.

H. Chad Lane and Kurt VanLehn. 2003. Coached program planning: dialogue-based support for novice program design. *SIGCSE Bull.*, 35(1):148–152.

Karen E. Lochbaum and Candace L Sidner. 1990. Models of plans to support communication: An initial report. In *Proceedings of the Eighth National Conference on Artificial Intelligence*, pages 485–490. AAAI Press.

A. Mitrović, P. Suraweera, B. Martin, and A. Weerasinghe. 2004. DB-Suite: Experiences with Three Intelligent, Web-Based Database Tutors. *Journal of Interactive Learning Research*, 15(4):409–433.

R. Ploetzner, P. Dillenbourg, M. Preier, and D. Traum. 1999. Learning by explaining to oneself and to others. *Collaborative learning: Cognitive and computational approaches*, pages 103–121.

M. D. Rekrut. 1992. Teaching to learn: Cross-age tutoring to enhance strategy instruction. *American Education Research Association*.

Rod D. Roscoe and Michelene T. H. Chi. 2007. Understanding tutor learning: Knowledge-building and knowledge-telling in peer tutors' explanations and questions. *Review of Educational Research*, 77(4):534–574.

Amy Soller. 2004. Computational modeling and analysis of knowledge sharing in collaborative distance learning. *User Modeling and User-Adapted Interaction*, Volume 14(4):351–381, January.

Kurt VanLehn, Pamela W. Jordan, Carolyn Penstein Rosé, Dumisizwe Bhembe, Michael Böttner, Andy Gaydos, Maxim Makatchev, Umarani Pappuswamy, Michael A. Ringenberg, Antonio Roque, Stephanie Siler, and Ramesh Srivastava. 2002. The architecture of why2-atlas: A coach for qualitative physics essay writing. In *ITS '02: Proceedings of the 6th International Conference on Intelligent Tutoring Systems*, pages 158–167, London, UK. Springer-Verlag.

Aurora Vizcaíno. 2005. A simulated student can improve collaborative learning. *International Journal of Artificial Intelligence in Education*, 15(1):3–40.

Marilyn Walker and Steve Whittaker. 1990. Mixed initiative in dialogue: an investigation into discourse segmentation. In *Proceedings of the 28th annual meeting on Association for Computational Linguistics*, pages 70–78, Morristown, NJ, USA. Association for Computational Linguistics.

Kai Warendorf and Colin Tan. 1997. Adis-an animated data structure intelligent tutoring system or putting an interactive tutor on the www. In *Intelligent Educational Systems on the World Wide Web (Workshop Proceedings), at the Eight International Conference on Artficial Intellignece in Education*.

Ian H. Witten and Eibe Frank. 2005. *Data Mining: Practical machine learning tools and techniques*. Morgan Kaufmann, San Francisco.

Using First and Second Language Models to Correct Preposition Errors in Second Language Authoring

Matthieu Hermet
School of Information Technology and Engineering
University of Ottawa
800, King Edward, Ottawa, Canada
mhermet@site.uottawa.ca

Alain Désilets
Institute for Information Technology

National Research Council of Canada
Bldg M-50, Montreal Road, Ottawa, K1A 0R6, Canada
alain.desilets@nrc-cnrc.gc.ca

Abstract

In this paper, we investigate a novel approach to correcting grammatical and lexical errors in texts written by second language authors. Contrary to previous approaches which tend to use unilingual models of the user's second language (L2), this new approach uses a simple roundtrip Machine Translation method which leverages information about both the author's first (L1) and second languages. We compare the repair rate of this roundtrip translation approach to that of an existing approach based on a unilingual L2 model with shallow syntactic pruning, on a series of preposition choice errors. We find no statistically significant difference between the two approaches, but find that a hybrid combination of both does perform significantly better than either one in isolation. Finally, we illustrate how the translation approach has the potential of repairing very complex errors which would be hard to treat without leveraging knowledge of the author's L1.

1 Introduction

In this paper, we investigate a novel approach to correcting grammatical and lexical errors in texts written by second language learners or authors. Contrary to previous approaches which tend to use unilingual models of the user's second language (L2), this new approach uses a translation model based on both the user's first (L1) and second languages. It has the advantage of being able to model linguistic interference phenomena, that is, errors which are produced through literal translation from the author's first language. Although we apply this method in the context of French-as-a-Second-Language, its principles are largely independent of language, and could also be extended to other classes of errors. Note that this is preliminary work which, in a first step, focuses on error correction, and ignores for now the preliminary step of error detection which is left for future research.

This work is of interest to applications in Computer-Assisted-Language-Learning (CALL) and Intelligent Tutoring Systems (ITS), where tutoring material often consists of drills such as fill-in-the-blanks or multiple-choice-questions. These require very little use of a learner's language production capacities, and in order to support richer free-text assessment capabilities, ITS systems thus need to use error detection and correction functionalities (Heift and Schulze, 2007).

Editing Aids (EA) are tools which assist a user in producing written compositions. They typically use rules for grammar checking as well as lexical heuristics to suggest stylistic tips, synonyms or fallacious collocations. Advanced examples of such

Proceedings of the NAACL HLT Workshop on Innovative Use of NLP for Building Educational Applications, pages 64–72,
Boulder, Colorado, June 2009. ©2009 Association for Computational Linguistics

tools include Antidote[1] for French and StyleWriter[2] for English. Text Editors like MS Word and Word Perfect also include grammar checkers, but their style checking capabilities tend to be limited. All these tools can provide useful assistance to editing style, but they were not designed to assist with many errors found typically in highly non-idiomatic sentences produced by L2 authors.

Recent work in the field of error correction, especially as applied to English in the context of English as a Second Language (ESL), show an increasing use of corpora and language models. These have the advantage of offering a model of correctness based on common usage, independently of any meta-information on correctness. Corpus-based approaches are also able to correct higher level lexical-syntactic errors, such as the choice of preposition which is often semantically governed by other parts of the sentence.

The reminder of this paper is organized as follows. In section 2, we give a detailed account of the problem of preposition errors in a Second Language Learning (SLL) context. Related work is reviewed in section 3 and the algorithmic framework is presented in section 4. An evaluation is discussed in section 5, and conclusions and directions for future research are presented in section 6.

2 The Preposition Problem

Prepositions constitute 14% of all tokens produced in most languages (Fort & Guillaume 2007). They are reported as yielding among the highest error class rates across various languages (Izumi, 2004, for Japanese, Granger et al., 2001, for French). In their analysis of a small corpus of advanced-intermediate French as a Second Language (FSL) learners, Hermet et al. (2008) found that preposition choice accounted for 17.2 % of all errors. Prepositions can be seen as a special class of cognates, in the sense that the same L1 preposition used in different L1 sentences, could translate to several different L2 prepositions.

Automatic error detection/correction methods often process prepositions and determiners in the same way because they both fall in the class of function-words. However, one can make the argument that preposition errors deserve a different and deeper kind of treatment, because they tend to be more semantically motivated (event hough some prepositions governed by verbs draw a purely functional relation). In contrast, determiners are not semantically motivated and only vary on the register of quantity (or genre in some languages).

For example, there are 37 determiners in French, most of which can be used interchangeably without significantly affecting the syntax of a sentence, and often, not even its meaning ("I'll have one coffee"/"I'll have a coffee"/"I'll have some coffee"/"I'll have my coffee"/"I'll have coffee" are all rather alike). Comparatively, there are 85 simple prepositions and 222 compounds ones and they cannot be used interchangeably without significantly modifying the sense of an utterance, except for cases of synonymy.

In this paper, we focus our attention on preposition correction only, as it seems to be a more complex problem than determiners. While in principle the methods described here could handle determiner errors, we feel that our framework, which involves parsing in combination with a very large language model and Machine Translation, constitutes heavier machinery than is warranted for that simpler problem.

There are two major causes of preposition errors in a SLL context. The first kind is caused by lexical confusion within the second language itself. For example, a L2 author writing in English may erroneously use a location preposition like *"at"* where another location preposition like *"in"* would have been more appropriate. The second kind involves linguistic interference between prepositions in L1 and prepositions in L2 (Granger et al., 2001). For example, a Second Language Learner who wants to render the following two English sentences in French *"I go to Montreal"* and *"I go to Argentina"*, might use the same French preposition *"à"* for *"to"*, when in fact, French usage dictates that you write *"à Montréal"*, and *"en Argentine"*. Note that the situation varies greatly from language to language. The same two English sentences rendered in Italian and German would in fact employ a same preposition, whereas in Spanish, different prepositions would also be required as in French.

[1] www.druide.com
[2] www.stylewriter-usa.com

Studies have found that the majority of errors made by L2 authors (especially intermediate to advanced ones) are caused by such linguistic interference (Wang and Garigliano, 1992, Cowan, 1983, p 109). Note that this kind of linguistic interference can often lead to much more severe and hard to repair errors, as illustrated by the following example, taken from an actual SLL corpus. Say a native English author wants to render *"Police arrived at the scene of the crime"* into French (her L2). Because she is not fluent in French, she translates the last part of the sentence to *"à la scène de la crime"*. This literal translation turns out to be highly unidiomatic in French, and should instead be written as *"sur les lieux du crime"* (which in English, would translate literally to *"on the location of the crime"*).

One might suspect that preposition errors of the first type would be solvable using unilingual L2 language models, but that the second type might benefit from a language model which also takes L1 into account. This is the main question investigated in this paper.

3 Related Work

Historically, grammatical error correction has been done through parsing-based techniques such as syntactic constraint-relaxation (L'haire & Vandeventer-Feltin, 2003), or mal-rules modeling (Schneider and McCoy, 1998). But generating the rule-bases needed by these types of approaches involves a lot of manual work, and may still in the end be too imprecise to convey information on the nature and solution of an error. Recently, more effort has been put in methods that rely on automatically built language models. Typically, this kind of work will focus either on a restricted class of errors or on specific domains. Seneff and Lee (2006) propose a two-phased generation-based framework where a n-gram model re-ranked by a stochastic context-free-grammar model is used to correct sentence-level errors in the language domain of flight reservation. Brockett et al. (2006) used a Brown noise channel translation model to record patterns of determiner error correction on a small set of mass-nouns, and reducing the error spectrum in both class and semantic domain, but adding detection capabilities. Note that although they use a translation model, it processes only text that is in one language. More specifically, the system learned to "translate" from poorly written English into correctly written English.

Chodorow et al. (2007) employed a maximum entropy model to estimate the probability of 34 prepositions based on 25 local context features ranging from words to NP/VP chunks. They use lemmatization as a means of generalization and trained their model over 7 million prepositional contexts, achieving results of 84% precision and 19% recall in preposition error detection in the best of the system's configurations. Gamon et al. (2008) worked on a similar approach using only tagged trigram left and right contexts: a model of prepositions uses serves to identify preposition errors and the Web provides examples of correct form. They evaluate their framework on the task of preposition identification and report results ranging from 74 to 45% precision on a set of 13 prepositions.

Yi et al. (2008) use the Web as corpus and send segments of sentences of varying length as bag-of-constituents queries to retrieve occurrence contexts. The number of the queried segments is a PoS condition of "check-points" sensitive to typical errors made by L2 authors. The contexts retrieved are in turn analyzed for correspondence with the original input. The detection and correction methods differ according to the class of the error. Determiner errors call for distinct detection and correction procedures while collocation errors use the same procedure for both. Determiner errors are discovered by thresholds ratios on search hits statistics, taking into account probable ambiguities, since multiple forms of determiners can be valid in a single context. Collocation errors on the other hand, are assessed only by a threshold on absolute counts, that is, a form different from the input automatically signals an error and provides its correction. This suggests that detection and correction procedures coincide when the error ceases to bear on a function word.

Similarly, Hermet et al. (2008) use a Web as corpus based approach to address the correction of preposition errors in a French-as-a-Second-Language (FSL) context. Candidate prepositions are substituted for erroneous ones following a taxonomy of semantic classes, which produces a set of alternate sentences for each error. The main interest of their study is the use of a syntax-based sentence generalization method to maximize the likelihood that at least one of the alternatives will have at least one hits on the Web. They achieve accuracy of 69% in error repair (no error detection), on a small set of clauses written by FSL Learners.

Very little work has been done to actually exploit knowledge of a L2 author's first language, in correcting errors. Several authors (Wang and Garigliano, 1992, Anderson, 1995, La Torre, 1999, Somers, 2001) have suggested that students may learn by analyzing erroneous sentences produced by a MT system, and reflecting on the probable cause of errors, especially in terms of interference between the two languages. In this context however, the MT system is used only to generate exercises, as opposed to helping the student find and correct errors in texts that he produces.

Although it is not based on an MT model, Wang and Garigliano propose an algorithm which uses a hand-crafted, domain-specific, mixed L1 and L2 grammar, in order to identify L1 interference errors in L2 sentences. L2 sentences are parsed with this mixed grammar, giving priority to L2 rules, and only employing L1 rules as a last resort. Parts of the sentence which required the user of L1 rules are labeled as errors caused by L1 interference. The paper does not present an actual evaluation of the algorithm.

Finally, a patent by Dymetman and Isabelle (2005) describes several ways in which MT technology could be used to correct L2 errors, but to our knowledge, none of them has been implemented and evaluated yet.

4 Algorithmic Framework

As discussed in section 2, L2 authoring errors can be caused by confusions within the L2 itself, or by linguistic interference between L1 and L2. In order to account for this duality, we investigate the use of two correction strategies, one which is based on unilingual models of L2, and one which is based on translation models between L1 and L2.

Input Sentence

Il y a une grande fenêtre qui permet au soleil <à> entrer

(there is a large window which lets the sun come in)

Syntactic Pruning and Lemmatization

permettre <à> entrer

(let come in)

Generation of alternate prepositions

semantically related: *dans, en, chez, sur, sous, au, dans, après, avant, en, vers*

most common: *de, avec, par, pour*

Query and sort alternative phrases

permettre d'entrer: 119 000 hits
permettre avant entrer: 12 hits
permettre à entrer: 4 hits
permettre en entrer: 2 hits

...

→ preposition <*d'*> is returned as correction

Figure 1. Typical processing carried out by the *Unilingual* approach.

The first approach, called the *Unilingual* strategy, is illustrated by the example in Figure 1. It uses a web search engine (Yahoo) as a simple, unilingual language model, where the probability of a L2 phrase is estimated simply by counting its number of occurrences in Web pages of that language. A severe limitation of this kind of model is that it can only estimate the probability of phrases that appear at least once on the Web. In contrast, an N-gram model (for example) is able to estimate the probability of phrases that it has never seen in the training corpus. In order to deal with this limitation, syntactic pruning is therefore applied to the phrase before it is sent to the search engine, in order to eliminate parts which are not core to the context of use of the preposition, thus increasing the odds that the pruned sentence will have at least one occurrence on the Web.

This pruning and generalization is done by carrying out syntactic analysis with the Xerox Incremental Parser for the syntactic analysis (Ref XIP). XIP is an error robust, symbolic, dependency parser, which outputs syntactic information at the constituency and dependency levels. Its ability to produce syntactic analyses in the presence of errors is

Category	Prepositions
Localization	*in front, behind, after, before, above, in, at, on, below, above...*
Temporal	*at, in, after, before, for, during, since...*
Cause	*for, because of*
Goal	*for, at*
Manner	*in, by, with, according to...*
Material	*in, of*
Possession/Relation	*to, at, with respect to...*
Most common	*to, at, on, with, by, for*

Table 1. Categories of prepositions – the list is given in English, and non exhaustive for space reasons.

particularly interesting in the context of second language authoring where the sentences produced by the authors can be quite far from grammatical correctness. The input sentence is fed to the parser as two segments split at error point (in this case, at the location of the erroneous preposition). This ensures that the parses are correct and not affected at dependency level by the presence of error. The syntactic analyses are needed to perform syntactic pruning, which is a crucial step in our framework, following Hermet et. al (2008). Pruning is performed by way of chunking heuristics, which are controlled by grammatical features, provided by XIP's morphological analysis (PoS tagger). The heuristics are designed to suppress syntactically extraneous material in the sentence, such as adverbs, some adjectives and some NPs. Adverbs are removed in all cases, while adjectives are only removed when they are not in a position to govern a Prepositional Phrase. NPs are suppressed in controlled cases, based on the verb sub-categorization frame, when a PP can be attached directly to the preceding verb. In case of ambiguity in the attachment of the PP, two versions of the pruned sentence can be produced reflecting two different PP attachments. Lemmatization of verbs is also carried out in the pruning step.

After pruning, the right and left sides of the sentences are re-assembled with alternate prepositions. The replacement of prepositions is controlled by way of semantics. Since prepositions are richer in sense than strict function words, they can therefore be categorized according to semantics. Saint-Dizier (2007) proposes such a taxonomy, and in our framework, prepositions have been grouped in 7 non-exclusive categories. Table 1 provides details of this categorization. The input preposition is mapped to all the sets it belongs to, and corresponding alternates are retrieved as correction candidates. The 6 most frequent French preposition are also added automatically to the candidates list.

The resulting sentences are then sent to the Yahoo Search Engine and hits are counted. The number of hits returned by each of the queries is used as decision criteria, and the preposition contained in the query with the most hits is selected as the correction candidate.

While the above *Unilingual* strategy might work for simple cases of L1 interference, one would not expect it to work as well in more complex cases where both the preposition and its governing parts have been translated too literally. For example, in the case of the example from section 2, while the *Unilingual* strategy might be able to effect correction *"**sur** la scène du crime"* which is marginally better than the original *"**à** la scène du crime"* (12K hits versus 1K), it cannot address the root of the problem, that is, the unidiomatic expression *"scène du crime"* which should instead be rendered as *"lieux du crime"* (38K hits). In this particular case, it is not really an issue because it so happens that *"sur"* is the correct preposition to use for both *"lieux du crime"* and *"scène du crime"*, but in our experience, that is not always the case. Note also that the *Unilingual* approach can only deal with preposition errors (although it would be easy enough to extend it to other kinds of function words), and cannot deal with more semantically deep L1 interference.

To address these issues, we experimented with a second strategy which we will refer to as the *Roundtrip Machine Translation* approach (or *Roundtrip MT* for short). Note that our approach is different from that of Brockett et al. (2006), as we do make use of a truly multi-lingual translation model. In contrast, Brockett's translation model was trained on texts that were written in the same language, with the sources being ill-written text in the same language as the properly-formed target texts. One drawback of our approach however is that it may require different translation models for speakers with different first languages.

There are many ways in which error-correction could be carried out using MT techniques. Several of these have been described in a patent by Dymetman and Isabelle (2005), but to our knowledge, none of them have yet been implemented and evaluated. In this paper, we use the simplest possible implementation of this concept, namely, we carry out a single round-trip translation. Given a potentially erroneous L2 sentence written by a second language author, we translate it to the author's L1 language, and then back to L2. Even with this simple approach, we often find that errors which were present in the original L2 sentence have been repaired in the roundtrip version. This may sound surprising, since one would expect the roundtrip sentence to be worse than the original, on account of the "Chinese Whisper" effect. Our current theory for why this is not the case in practice goes as follows. In the course of translating the original L2 sentence to L1, when the MT system encounters a part that is ill-formed, it will tend to use single word entries from its phrase table, because longer phrases will not have been represented in the well-formed L2 training data. In other words, the system tends to generate a word for word translation of ill-formed parts, which mirrors exactly what L2 authors do when they write poorly formed L2 sentences by translating too literally from their L1 thought. As a result, the L1 sentence produced by the MT system is often well formed for that language. Subsequently, when the MT system tries to translate that well-formed L1 sentence back to L2, it is therefore able to use longer entries from its phrase table, and hence produce a better L2 translation of that part than what the author originally produced.

We use Google Translate as a translation engine for matter of simplicity. A drawback of using such an online service is that it is essentially a closed box, and we therefore have little control over the translation process, and no access to lower level data generated by the system in the course of translation (e.g. phrase alignments between source and target sentences). In particular, this means that we can only generate one alternative L2 sentence, and have no way of assessing which parts of this single alternative have a high probability of being better than their corresponding parts in the original L2 sentence written by the author. In other words, we have no way of telling which changes are likely to be false positives, and which changes are likely to be true positives. This is the main reason why we focus only on error repair in this preliminary work.

The roundtrip sentences generated with Google Translate often differ significantly from the original L2 sentence, and in more ways than just the erroneous preposition used by the author. For example, the (pruned) clause *"avoir du succès **en** le recrutement" ("to be successful **in** recruiting"*) might come back as as *"réussir **à** recruter" ("to succeed **in** recruiting"*). Here, the translation is acceptable, but the preposition used by the MT system is not appropriate for use in the original sentence as written by the L2 author. Conversely, a roundtrip translation can be ill-formed, yet use a preposition which would be correct in the original L2 sentence. For example, *"regarder **à** des films" ("look at some movies"*) might come back as *"inspecter des films" ("inspect some films"*). Here, the original meaning is somewhat lost, but the system correctly suggested that there should be no preposition before *"des films"*.

Hence, in the context of the *Roundtrip MT* approach, we need two ways of measuring appropriateness of the suggested corrections for given clauses. The first approach, which we call the *Clause* criteria, looks at whether or not the whole clause has been restored to a correct idiomatic form (including correct use of preposition) which also preserves the meaning intended by the author of the original sentence. Hence, according to this approach, an MT alternative may be deemed correct, even if it chooses a preposition which would have been incorrect if substituted in the original L2 sentence as is. In the second approach, called the *Prep* criteria, we only look at whether the preposition used by the MT system in the roundtrip translation, corresponds to the correct preposition to be used in the original L2 clause. Hence, with this approach, an MT alternative may be deemed correct, even if the preposition chosen by the MT system is actually inappropriate in the context of the generated roundtrip translation, or, even worse, if the roundtrip modified the clause to a point where it actually means something different than what the author actually intended.

Of course, in the case of the *Prep* evaluation criteria, having the MT system return a sentence which employs the proper preposition to use in the context of the original L2 sentence is not the end of the process. In an error correction context, one must also isolate the correct preposition and insert it in the appropriate place in the original L2 sentence. This part of the processing chain is not currently implemented, but would be easy to do, if we used an MT system that provided us with the alignment information between the source sentence and the target sentence generated. The accuracy figures which we present in this paper assume that this mapping has been implemented and that this particular part of the process can be done with 100% accuracy (a claim which, while plausible, still needs to be demonstrated in future work).

We also investigate a third strategy called *Hybrid*, which uses the *Roundtrip MT* approach as a backup for cases where the *Unilingual* approach is unable to distinguish between different choices of preposition. The latter typically occurs when the system is not able to sufficiently prune and generalize the phrase, resulting in a situation where all pruned variants yield zero hits on the Web, no matter what preposition is used. One could of course also use the *Unilingual* approach as a backup for the *Roundtrip MT* approach, but this would be harder to implement since the MT system always returns an answer, and our use of the online Google Translate system precludes any attempt to estimate the confidence level of that answer.

In conclusion to this section, we use three preposition correction strategies: *Unilingual*, *Roundtrip MT* and *Hybrid*, and in the case of the *Roundtrip MT* approach, appropriateness of the corrections can be evaluated using two criteria: *Prep* and *Clause*.

5 Evaluation and Results

5.1 Corpus and Evaluation Metric

For evaluation, we extracted clauses containing preposition errors from a small corpus of texts written by advanced-intermediate French as a Second Language (FSL) student in the course of one semester. The corpus contained about 50, 000 words and 133 unique preposition errors. While relatively small, we believe this set to be sufficiently rich to test the approach. Most clauses also presented other errors, including orthographic, tense, agreement, morphologic and auxiliary errors, of which only the last two affect parsing. The clauses were fed as is to the correction algorithms, without first fixing the other types of errors. But to our surprise, XIP's robust parsing has proven resistant in that it produced enough information to enable correct pruning based on chunking information, and we report no pruning errors. Chodorow et al. (2008) stress the importance of agreement between annotators when retrieving or correcting preposition errors. In our case, our policy has been to only retain errors reported by both authors of this paper, and correction of these errors has raised little matter of dispute.

Algorithm	Repair rate (%)
Unilingual	68.7
Roundtrip MT (Clause)	44.8
Roundtrip MT (Prep)	66.4
Hybrid (Prep)	82.1

Table 2. Results for 3 algorithms on 133 sentences.

We evaluated the various algorithms in terms of repair rate, that is, the percentage of times that the algorithm proposed an appropriate fix (the absence of a suggestion was taken to be an inappropriate fix). These figures are reported in Table 2.

5.2 Discussion

ANOVA of the data summarized in Table 2 reveals a statistically significant ($p < 0.001$) effect of the algorithm on repair rate. Although *Roundtrip MT* performed slightly worse than *Unilingual* (66.4% versus 68.7%), this difference was not found to be statistically significant. On one hand, we found that round-trip translation sometimes result in spectacular restorations of long and clumsy phrases caused by complex linguistic interference. However, too often the Chinese whispers effect destroyed the sense of the original phrase, resulting in inappropriate suggestions. This is evidenced by the fact that repair rate of the *Roundtrip MT* approach was significantly lower ($p < 0.001$) when using the

Clause criteria (44.8%) than when using the *Prep* criteria (66.4%). It seems that, in the case of preposition correction, roundtrip MT is best used as a way to to generate an L2 alternative from which to mine the correct preposition. Indeed, flawed as they are, these distorted roundtrip segments corrected prepositions errors in 66.4% of the cases. However, for a full picture, the approach should be tried on more data, and on other classes of errors. Particularly, we currently lack sufficient data to test the hypothesis that the approach could address the correction of more complex literal translations by SL Learners.

In the *Unilingual* approach, the Yahoo Web search engine proved to be an insufficient language model for 31 cases out of 133, meaning that even the pruned and generalized phrases got zero hits, no matter what alternative preposition was used. In those cases, the *Hybrid* approach would then attempt correction using *MT Roundtrip* approach. This turned out to work quite well, since it resulted in an overall accuracy of 82.1%. ANOVA on the data for *Hybrid* and the two pure approaches reveals a significant effect ($p < 0.001$) of the algorithm factor. Individual t-tests between the *Hybrid* approach and each of the two pure approaches also reveal statistically significant differences ($p < 0.001$). The improvements provided by the hybrid approach are fairly substantial, and represent relative gains of 19.5% over the pure *Unilingual* approach, and 23.6% over the pure *Roundtrip MT* approach. The success of this combined approach might be attributable to the fact that the two approaches follow different paradigms. *Roundtrip MT* uses a model of controlled incorrectness (errors of anglicism) and *Unilingual* a model of correctness (occurrences of correct forms). In this respect, the relatively low agreement between the two approaches (65.4%) is not surprising.

6 Conclusion and Future Work

In this paper, we have demonstrated for the first time that a bilingual Machine Translation approach can be used to good effect to correct errors in texts written by Second Language Authors or Learners. In the case of preposition error correction we found that, while the MT approach on its own did not perform significantly better than a unilingual approach, a hybrid combination of both performed much better than the unilingual approach alone. More work needs to be carried out in order to fully evaluate the potential of the MT approach. In particular, we plan to experiment with this kind of approach to deal with more complex cases of L1 interference which result in severely damaged L2 sentences.

In this paper, we compared the bilingual MT approach to a unilingual baseline which used a relatively simple Web as a corpus algorithm, whose accuracy is comparable to that reported in the literature for a similar preposition correction algorithm (Yi et al, 2008). Notwithstanding the fact that such simple Web as a corpus approaches have often been shown to be competitive with (if not better than) more complex algorithms which cannot leverage the full extent of the web (Halevy et al., 2009), it would be interesting to compare the bilingual MT approach to more sophisticated unilingual algorithms for preposition correction, many of which are referenced in section 3.

Error *detection* is another area for future research. In this paper, we limited ourselves to error correction, since it could be solved through a very simple round-trip translation, without requiring a detailed control of the MT system, or access to lower level information generated by the system in the course of translation (for example, intermediate hypotheses with probabilities and alignment information between source and target sentences). In contrast, we believe that error detection with an MT approach will require this kind of finer control and access to the guts of the MT system. We plan to investigate this using the PORTAGE MT system (Ueffing et al., 2007). Essentially, we plan to use the MT system's internal information to assign confidence scores to various segments of the roundtrip translation, and label them as corrections if this confidence is above a certain threshold. In doing this, we will be following in the footsteps of Yi et al. (2008) who use the same algorithm for error detection and error correction. The process of detecting an error is simply one of determining whether the system's topmost alternative is different from what appeared in the original sentence, and whether the system's confidence in that alternative is sufficiently high to take the risk of presenting it to the user as a suggested correction.

Acknowledgments

The authors are indebted to the following people (all from NRC) for helpful advice on how to best exploit MT for second language correction: Pierre Isabelle, George Foster and Eric Joanis.

References

Anderson, D. D. 1995. *Machine Translation As a Tool in Second Language Learning*. CALICO Journal, v13 n1 p68-97.

Brockett C., Dolan W. B., and Gamon M.. 2006. *Correcting ESL errors using phrasal SMT techniques*. In Proc. 21st International Conf. On Computational Linguistics and the 44th annual meeting of the ACL, p. 249–256, Sydney, Australia.

Chodorow M., Tetreault J. R. and Han N.-R.. 2007. *Detection of Grammatical Errors Involving Prepositions*. In Proc. ACL-SIGSEM Workshop on Prepositions. Prague, Czech Republic.

Cowan, J. R. 1983. *Towards a Psychological Theory of Interference in Second Language Learning*. In Second Language Learning: Contrastive Analysis, Error Analysis, and Related Aspects, edited by B. W. Robinett, J. Schachter, pp 109-119, The Univ. of Michigan Press.

Dymetman M., Isabelle, P. 2007. *Second language writing advisor*. US Patent #20070033002 , Feb 8, 2007.

Fort K., Guillaume B. 2007. *PrepLex: un lexique des prépositions du français pour l'analyse syntaxique*. TALN 2007, Toulouse, June 5-8.

Gamon M., Gao J. F., Brockett C., Klementiev A., Dolan W. B., and Vanderwende L. 2008. *Using contextual speller techniques and language modeling for ESL error correction*. In Proceedings of IJCNLP 2008, Hyderabad, India, January.

Granger S., Vandeventer A. & Hamel M. J. 2001. *Analyse de corpus d'apprenants pour l'ELAO basé sur le TAL*. TAL 42(2), 609-621.

Halevy, A., Norvig, P., Pereira, F. 2009. *"The Unreasonable Effectiveness of Data."*, IEEE Intelligent Systems, March/April 2009, pp 8-12.

Heift, T. & Schulze, M. 2007. *Errors and Intelligence in Computer-Assisted Language Learning: Parsers and Pedagogues*. Routledge.

Hermet, M., Désilets, A., Szpakowicz, S. 2008. *Using the Web as a Linguistic Resource to Automatically Correct Lexico-Syntactic Errors*. In Proceedings of the LREC'08. Marrakech, Morroco.

Izumi, E., K. Uchimoto, and H. Isahara. 2004. *The overview of the sst speech corpus of Japanese learner English and evaluation through the experiment on automatic detection of learners' errors*. In LREC.

La Torre, M. D. 1999. *A web-based resource to imprive translation skills*. ReCALL, Vol 11, No3, pp. 41-49.

Lee J. and Seneff S. 2006. *Automatic grammar correction for second-language learners*. In Interspeech. ICSLP. p. 1978-1981. Pittsburgh.

L'haire S. & Vandeventer Faltin A. 2003. *Error diagnosis in the FreeText project*. CALICO 20(3), 481-495, special Issue Error Analysis and Error Correction in Computer-Assisted Language Learning, T. Heift & M. Schulze (eds.).

Schneider, D. and McCoy, K. F. 1998. *Recognizing syntactic errors in the writing of second language learners*. In Proceedings of COLING/ACL 98.

Saint-Dizier, P. 2007. *Regroupement des Prépositions par sens*. Undated Report. IRIT. Toulouse. http://www.irit.fr/recherches/ILPL/Site-Equipe/publi_fichier/prepLCS.doc

Somers, Harold. 2001. *Three Perspectives on MT in the Classroom*, MT SUMMIT VIII Workshop on Teaching Machine Translation, Santiago de Compostela, pages 25-29.

Tetreault J. and Chodorow M. 2008. *The Ups and Downs of Preposition Error Detection. COLING*, Manchester.

Ueffing, N., Simard, M., Larkin, S., Johnson, J. H. (2007), NRC's PORTAGE system for WMT 2007, ACL-2007 Workshop on SMT, Prague, Czech Republic 2007.

Wang, Y. and Garigliano, R. 1992. *An Intelligent Language Tutoring System for Handling Errors caused by Transfer*. In Proceedings of ITS-92, pp. 395-404.

Yi X., Gao J. F., Dolan W. B., 2008. *A Web-based English Proofing System for English as a Second Language Users*. In Proceedings of IJCNLP 2008, Hyderabad, India, January.

User Input and Interactions on *Microsoft Research ESL Assistant*

Claudia Leacock
Butler Hill Group
P.O. Box 935
Ridgefield, CT, 06877, USA
claudia.leacock@gmail.com

Michael Gamon
Microsoft Research
One Microsoft Way
Redmond, WA, 98052, USA
mgamon@microsoft.com

Chris Brockett
Microsoft Research
One Microsoft Way
Redmond, WA, 98052, USA
chrisbkt@microsoft.com

Abstract

ESL Assistant is a prototype web-based writing-assistance tool that is being developed for English Language Learners. The system focuses on types of errors that are typically made by non-native writers of American English. A freely-available prototype was deployed in June 2008. User data from this system are manually evaluated to identify writing domain and measure system accuracy. Combining the user log data with the evaluated rewrite suggestions enables us to determine how effectively English language learners are using the system, across rule types and across writing domains. We find that repeat users typically make informed choices and can distinguish correct suggestions from incorrect.

1 Introduction

Much current research in grammatical error detection and correction is focused on writing by English Language Learners (ELL). The *Microsoft Research ESL Assistant* is a web-based proofreading tool designed primarily for ELLs who are native speakers of East-Asian languages. Initial system development was informed by pre-existing ELL error corpora, which were used both to identify common ELL mistakes and to evaluate system performance. These corpora, however, were created from data collected under arguably artificial classroom or examination conditions, leaving unresolved the more practical question as to whether the *ESL Assistant* can actually help a person who produced the text to improve their English language writing skills in course of more realistic everyday writing tasks.

In June of 2008, a prototype version of this system was made freely available as a web service[1]. Both the writing suggestions that visitors see and the actions that they then take are recorded. As these more realistic data begin to accumulate, we can now begin to answer the above question.

2 Related Work

Language learner error correction techniques typically fall into either of two categories: rule-based or data-driven. Eeg-Olofsson and Knutsson (2003) report on a rule-based system that detects and corrects preposition errors in non-native Swedish text. Rule-based approaches have also been used to predict definiteness and indefiniteness of Japanese noun phrases as a preprocessing step for Japanese to English machine translation (Murata and Nagao 1993; Bond et al, 1994; Heine, 1998), a task that is similar to the prediction of English articles. More recently, data-driven approaches have gained popularity and been applied to article prediction in English (Knight and Chander 1994; Minnen et al, 2000; Turner and Charniak 2007), to an array of Japanese learners' errors in English (Izumi et al, 2003), to verb errors (Lee and Seneff, 2008), and to article and preposition correction in texts written by non-native ELLs (Han et al, 2004, 2006; Nagata et al, 2005; Nagata et al, 2006; De Felice and Pulman, 2007; Chodorow et al, 2007; Gamon et al, 2008, 2009; Tetreault and Chodorow, 2008a).

---

[1] http://www.eslassistant.com

Proceedings of the NAACL HLT Workshop on Innovative Use of NLP for Building Educational Applications, pages 73–81,
Boulder, Colorado, June 2009.

Noun Related (61%)	Articles *(ML)*	We have just checked **the* our stock. life is **journey/a journey*, travel it well! I think it 's **a/the* best way to resolve issues like this.
	Noun Number	London is one of the most attractive **city/cities* in the world. You have to write down all the details of each **things/thing* to do. Conversion always takes a lot of **efforts/effort*.
	Noun Of Noun	Please send the **feedback of customer/customer feedback* to me by mail.
Preposition Related (27%)	Preposition *(ML)*	I'm **on* home today, call me if you have a problem. It seems ok and I did not pay much attention **on/to* it. Below is my contact, looking forward **your/to your* response, thanks!
	Verb and Preposition	Ben is involved **this/in* this transaction. I should **to ask/ask* a rhetorical question … But I'll think **it/about it* a second time.
Verb Related (10%)	Gerund / Infinitive *(ML)*	He got me **roll/to roll* up my sleeve and make a fist. On Saturday, I with my classmate went **eating/to eat*. After **get/getting* a visa, I want to study in New York.
	Auxiliary Verb *(ML)*	To learn English we should **be speak/speak* it as much as possible . Hope you will **happy/be happy* in Taiwan . what **is/do* you want to say?
	Verb formation	If yes, I will **attached/attach* and resend to Geoff . The time and setting are **display/displayed* at the same time. You had **order/ordered* 3 items … this time. I am really **hope/hoping* to visit UCLA.
	Cognate/Verb Confusion	We cannot **image/imagine* what the environment really is at the site of end user .
	Irregular Verbs	I **teached/taught* him all the things that I know …
Adj Related (2%)	Adjective Confusions	She is very **interesting/interested* in the problem. So **Korea/Korean* Government is intensively fostering trade . … and it is **much/much more* reliable than your Courier Service.
	Adjective order	Employing the **Chinese ancient/ancient Chinese* proverb, that is …

Table 1: ESL Assistant grammatical error modules. *ML* modules are machine learned.

3 ESL Assistant

ESL Assistant takes a hybrid approach that combines statistical and rule-based techniques. Machine learning is used for those error types that are difficult to identify and resolve without taking into account complex contextual interactions, like article and preposition errors. Rule-based approaches handle those error types that are amenable to simpler solutions. For example, a regular expression is sufficient for identifying when a modal is (incorrectly) followed by a tensed verb.

The output of all modules, both machine-learned and rule-based, is filtered through a very large language model. Only when the language model finds that the likelihood of the suggested rewrite is sufficiently larger than the original text is a suggestion shown to the user. For a detailed description of *ESL Assistant's* architecture, see Gamon et al (2008, 2009).

Although this and the systems cited in section 2 are designed to be used by non-native writers, system performance is typically reported in relation to native text – the prediction of a preposition, for example, will ideally be consistent with usage in native, edited text. An error is counted each time the system predicts a token that differs from the observed usage and a correct prediction is counted each time the system predicts the usage that occurs in the text. Although somewhat artificial, this approach to evaluation offers the advantages of being fully automatable and having abundant quantities

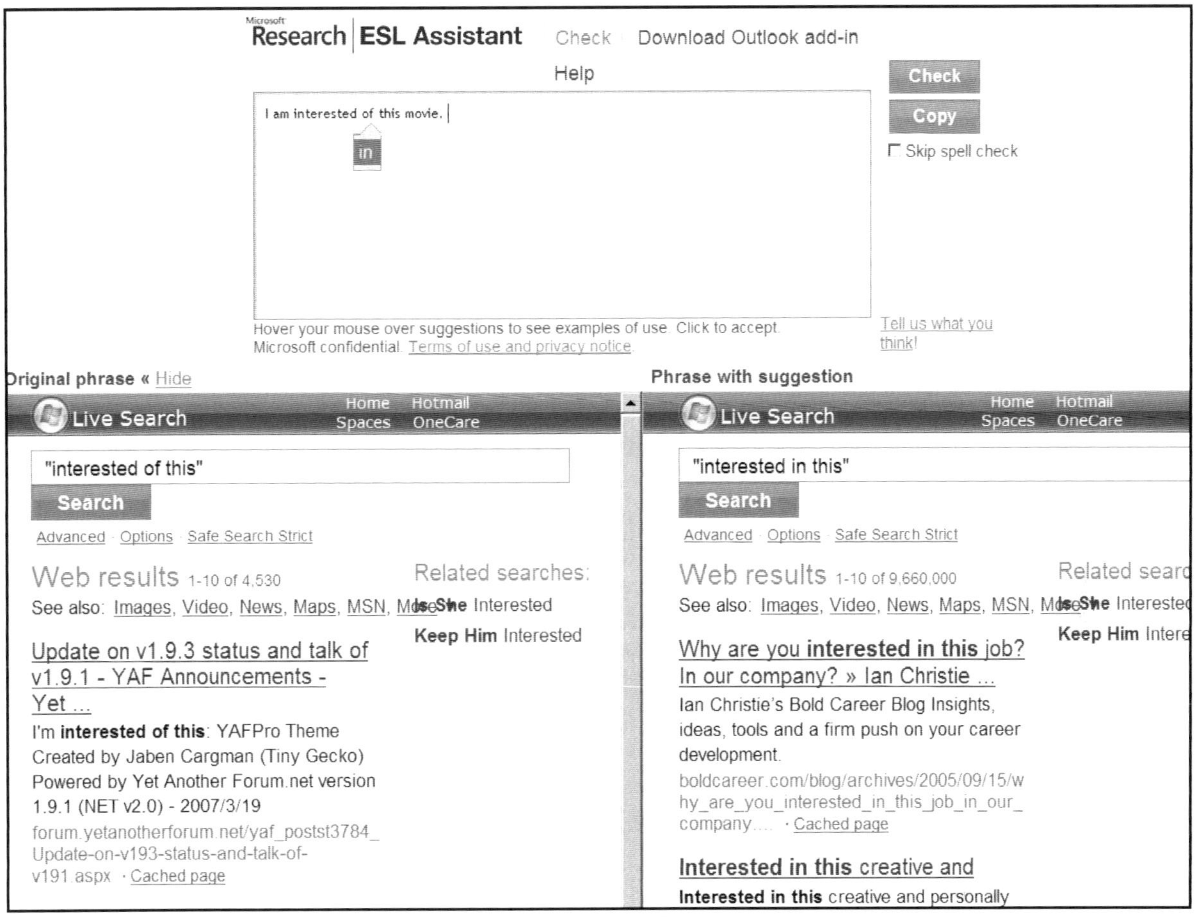

Figure 1: Screen shot of *ESL Assistant*

of edited data readily available. With respect to prepositions and articles, the *ESL Assistant's* classifiers achieve state-of-the-art performance when compared to results reported in the literature (Gamon et al, 2008), inasmuch as comparison is possible when the systems are evaluated on different samples of native text. For articles, the system had 86.76% accuracy as compared to 86.74% reported by Turner and Charniak (2007), who have the most recently reported results. For the harder problem of prepositions, *ESL Assistant's* accuracy is comparable to those reported by Tetreault and Chodorow (2008a) and De Felice and Pulman (2007).

3.1 Error Types

The ELL grammatical errors that *ESL Assistant* tries to correct were distilled from analysis of the most frequent errors made in Chinese and Japanese English language learner corpora (Gui and Yang, 2001; Izumi et al. 2004). The error types are shown in Table 1: modules identified with *ML* are machine-learned, while the remaining modules are rule-based. *ESL Assistant* does not attempt to identify those errors currently found by Microsoft Word™, such as subject/verb agreement.

ESL Assistant further contains a component to help address lexical selection issues. Since this module is currently undergoing major revision, we will not report on the results here.

3.2 System Development

Whereas evaluation on native writing is essential for system development and enables us to compare *ESL Assistant* performance with that of other reported results, it tells us little about how the system would perform when being used by its true target audience – non-native speakers of English engaged in real-life writing tasks. In this context, performance measurement inevitably entails manual evaluation, a process that is notoriously time consuming, costly and potentially error-prone. Human inter-rater agreement is known to be problematic on this task: it is likely to be high in the case of certain user error types, such as over-regularized verb inflection (where the system suggests replacing "writed" with "wrote"), but other error types are difficult to evaluate, and much may hinge upon who is performing the evaluation: Tetreault and Chodorow (2008b) report that for the annotation of preposition errors "using a single rater as a gold standard, there is the potential to over- or under-estimate precision by as much as 10%."

With these caveats in mind, we employed a single annotator to evaluate system performance on native data from the 1-million-word Chinese Learner's of English corpus (Gui and Yang, 2001; 2003). Half of the corpus was utilized to inform system development, while the remaining half was held back for "unseen" evaluation. While the absolute numbers for some modules are more reliable than for others, the relative change in numbers across evaluations has proven a beneficial yardstick of improved or degraded performance in the course of development.

3.3 The User Interface and Data Collection

Figure 1 shows the *ESL Assistant* user interface. When a visitor to the site types or pastes text into the box provided and clicks the "Check" button, the text is sent to a server for analysis. Any locations in the text that trigger an error flag are then displayed as underscored with a wavy line (known as a "squiggle"). If the user hovers the mouse over a squiggle, one or more suggested rewrites are displayed in a dropdown list. Then, if the user hovers over one of these suggestions, the system launches parallel web searches for both original and rewrite phrases in order to allow the user to compare real-word examples found on the World Wide Web. To accept a suggestion, the user clicks on the suggested rewrite, and the text is emended. Each of these actions, by both system and user, are logged on the server.

Since being launched in June, 2008, *ESL Assistant* has been visited over 100,000 times. Currently, the web page is being viewed between one to two thousand times every day. From these numbers alone it seems safe to conclude that there is much public interest in an ESL proofreading tool.

Fifty-three percent of visitors to the *ESL Assistant* web site are from countries in East Asia – its primary target audience – and an additional 15% are from the United States. Brazil, Canada, Germany, and the United Kingdom each account for about 2% of the site's visitors. Other countries represented in the database each account for 1% or less of all those who visit the site.

3.4 Database of User Input

User data are collected so that system performance can be evaluated on actual user input – as opposed to running pre-existing learner corpora through the system. User data provide invaluable insight into which rewrite suggestions users spend time viewing, and what action they subsequently take on the basis of those suggestions.

These data must be screened, since not all of the textual material entered by users in the web site is valid learner English language data. As with any publicly deployed web service, we find that numerous users will play with the system, entering nonsense strings or copying text from elsewhere on the website and pasting it into the text box.

To filter out the more obvious non-English data, we eliminate input that contains, for example, no alphabetic characters, no vowels/consonants in a sentence, or no white space. "Sentences" consisting of email subject lines are also removed, as are all the data entered by the *ESL Assistant* developers themselves. Since people often enter the same sentence many times within a session, we also remove repetitions of identical sentences within a single session.

Approximately 90% of the people who have visited the web site visit it once and never return. This behavior is far from unusual on the web, where site visits may have no clear purpose beyond idle curiosity. In addition, some proportion of visitors may in reality be automated "bots" that can be nearly indistinguishable from human visitors.

Nevertheless, we observe a significant number of repeat visitors who return several times to use the system to proofread email or other writing, and these are the users that we are intrinsically interested in. To measure performance, we therefore decided to evaluate on data collected from users who logged on and entered plausibly English-like text on at least four occasions. As of 2/10/2009, the frequent user database contained 39,944 session-unique sentences from 578 frequent users in 5,305 sessions.

Data from these users were manually annotated to identify writing domains as shown in Table 2. Fifty-three percent of the data consists of people proofreading email.[2] The dominance of email data is presumably due to an Outlook plug-in that is available on the web site, and automates copying email content into the tool. The non-technical domain consists of student essays, material posted on a personal web site, or employees writing about their company – for example, its history or processes. The technical writing is largely conference papers or dissertations in the fields of, for example, medicine and computer science. The "other" category includes lists and resumes (a writing style that deliberately omits articles and grammatical subjects), as well as text copied from online newspapers or other media and pasted in.

Writing Domain	Percent
Email	53%
Non-technical / essays	24%
Technical / scientific	14%
Other (lists, resumes, etc)	4%
Unrelated sentences	5%

Table 2: Writing domains of frequent users

Sessions categorized as "unrelated sentences" typically consist of a series of short, unrelated sentences that each contain one or more errors. These users are testing the system to see what it does. While this is a legitimate use of any grammar checker, the user is unlikely to be proofreading his or her writing, so these data are excluded from evaluation.

4 System Evaluation & User Interactions

We are manually evaluating the rewrite suggestions that *ESL Assistant* generated in order to determine both system accuracy and whether user acceptances led to an improvement in their writing. These categories are shown in Table 3. Note that results reported for non-native text look very different from those reported for native text (discussed in Section 3) because of the *neutral* categories which do not appear in the evaluation of native text. Systems reporting 87% accuracy on native text cannot achieve anything near that on

Evaluation	Subcategory: Description
Good	**Correct flag**: The correction fixes a problem in the user input.
Neutral	**Both Good**: The suggestion is a legitimate alternative to well-formed original input: *I like working/to work.*
	Misdiagnosis: the original input contained an error but the suggested rewrite neither improves nor further degrades the input: *If you ~~have~~ fail machine on hand.*
	Both Wrong: An error type is correctly diagnosed but the suggested rewrite does not correct the problem: *can you give me suggestion.* (suggests *the* instead of *a*)
	Non-ascii: A non-ascii or text markup character is in the immediate context.
Bad	**False Flag**: The suggestion resulted in an error or would otherwise lead to a degradation over the original user input.

Table 3: Evaluation categories

non-native ELL text because almost one third of the flags fall into a neutral category.

In 51% of the 39,944 frequent user sentences, the system generated at least one grammatical error flag, for a total of 17,832 flags. Thirteen percent of the time, the user ignored the flags. The remaining 87% of the flags were inspected by the user, and of those, the user looked at the suggested rewrites without taking further action 31% of the time. For 28% of the flags, the user hovered over a suggestion to trigger a parallel web search but did not accept the proposed rewrite. Nevertheless, 41% of inspected rewrites were accepted, causing the original string in the text to be revised. Overall, the users inspected about 15.5K suggested rewrites to accept about 6.4K. A significant number of users appear to be inspecting the suggested revisions and making deliberate choices to accept or not accept.

The next question is: Are users making the right choices? To help answer this question, 34% of the user sessions have been manually evaluated for system accuracy – a total of approximately 5.1K grammatical error flags. For each error category and for the three major writing domains, we:

[2] These are anonymized to protect user privacy.

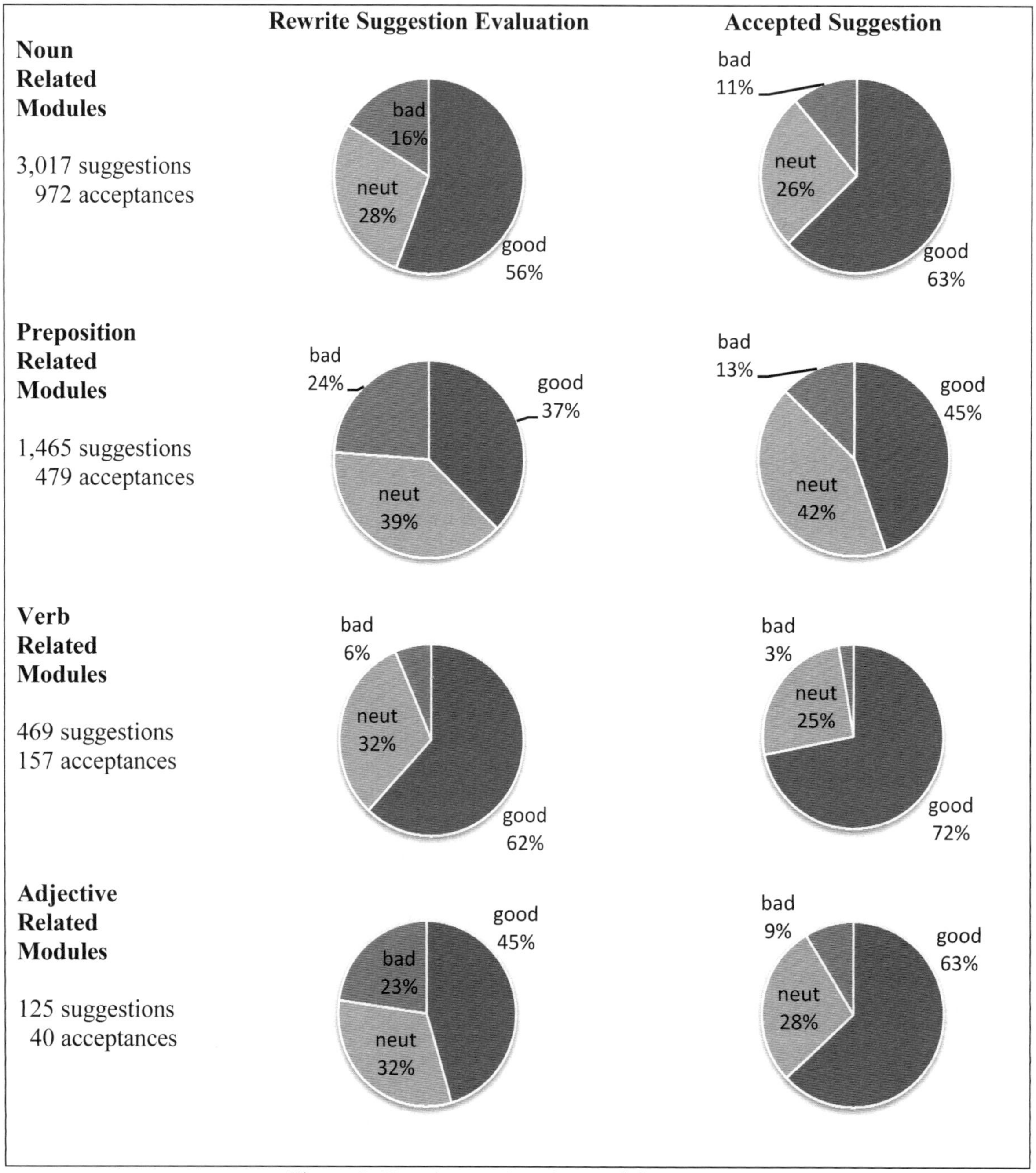

Figure 2: User interactions by module category

1. Calculated system accuracy for all flags, regardless of user actions.
2. Calculated system accuracy for only those rewrites that the user accepted
3. Compared the ratio of good to bad flags.

Results for the individual error categories are shown in Figure 2. Users consistently accept a greater proportion of good suggestions than they do bad ones across all error categories. This is most pronounced for the adjective-related modules, where the overall rate of good suggestions improved 17.6% after the user made the decision to accept a suggestion, while the system's false positive rate dropped 14.1% after the decision. For the noun-related modules, the system's most produc-

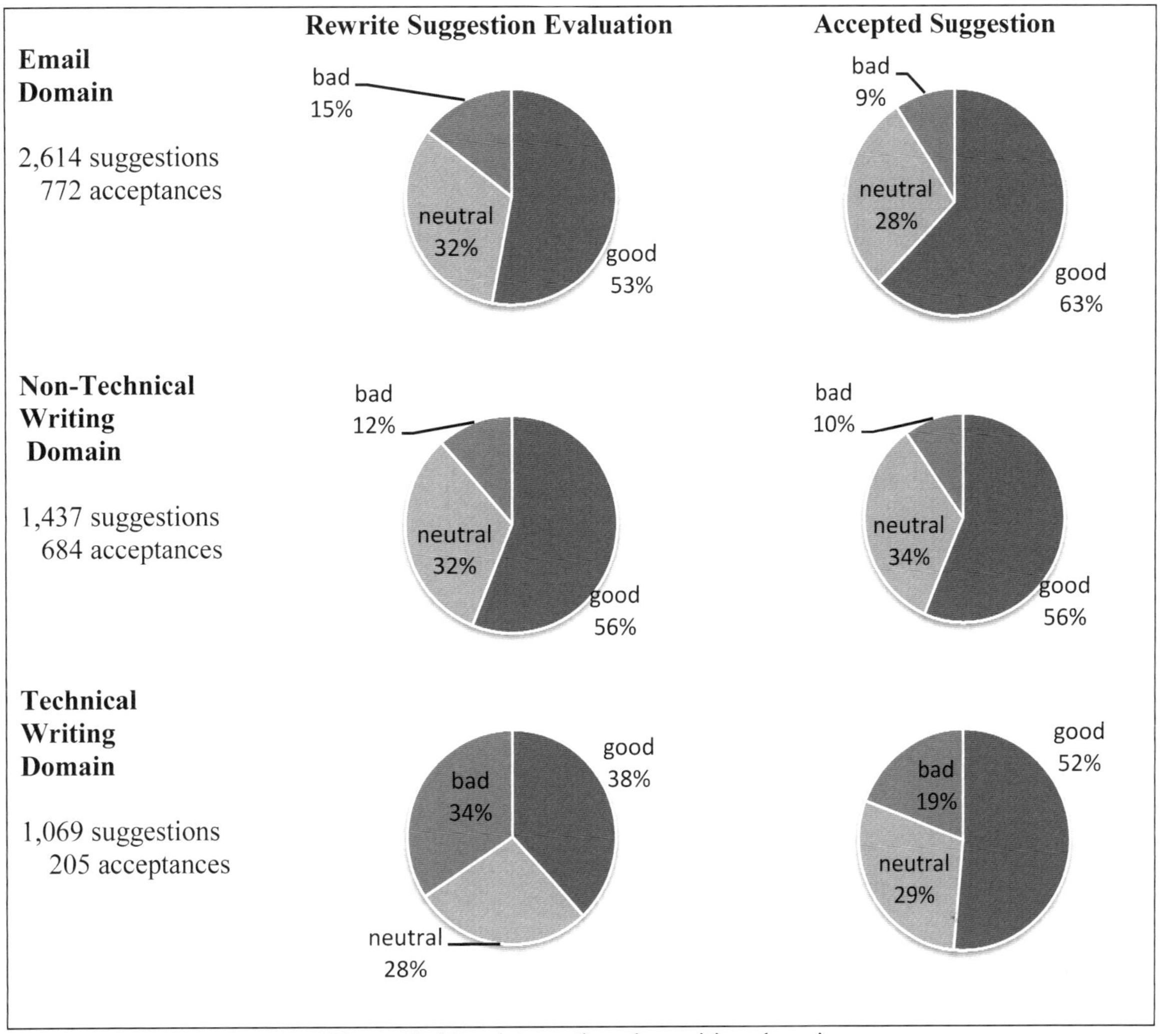

Figure 3: User interactions by writing domain

tive modules, the overall good flag rate increased by 7% while the false positive rate dropped 5%. All differences in false positive rates are statistically significant in Wilcoxon's signed-ranks test.

When all of the modules are evaluated across the three major writing domains, shown in figure 3, the same pattern of user discrimination between good and bad flags holds. This is most evident in the technical writing domain, where the overall rate of good suggestions improved 13.2% after accepting the suggestion and the false positive rate dropped 15.1% after the decision. It is least marked for the essay/nontechnical writing domain. Here the overall good flag rate increased by only .3% while the false positive rate dropped 1.6%. Again, all of the differences in false positive rates are statistically significant in Wilcoxon's signed-ranks test. These findings are consistent with those for the machine learned articles and prepositions modules in the email domain (Chodorow et al, *under review*).

A probable explanation for the differences seen across the domains is that those users who are proofreading non-technical writing are, as a whole, less proficient in English than the users who are writing in the other domains. Users who are proofreading technical writing are typically writing a dissertation or paper in English and therefore tend to relatively fluent in the language. The email domain comprises people who are confident enough in their English language skills to communicate with colleagues and friends by email in English. With the essay/non-technical writers, it often is not clear who the intended audience is. If there *is* any indication of audience, it is often an instructor. Users in this domain appear to be the least English-language proficient of the *ESL Assistant* users, so it is unsurprising that they are less effective in discriminating between good and bad flags than their more proficient counterparts. Thus it appears that those users who are most in need of the system are being helped by it least – an important direction for future work.

Finally, we look at whether the neutral flags, which account for 29% of the total flags, have any effect. The two neutral categories highlighted in Table 3, flags that either misdiagnose the error or that diagnose it but do not correct it, account for 74% of *ESL Assistant's* neutral flags. Although these suggested rewrites do not improve the sentence, they do highlight an environment that contains an error. The question is: What is the effect of identifying an error when the rewrite doesn't improve the sentence?

To estimate this, we searched for cases where *ESL Assistant* produced a neutral flag and, though the user did not accept the suggestion, a revised sentence that generated no flag was subsequently submitted for analysis. For example, one user entered: "This early morning i got a from head office ...". *ESL Assistant* suggested deleting *from*, which does not improve the sentence. Subsequently, in the same session, the user submitted, "This early morning I heard from the head office ..." In this instance, the system correctly identified the location of an error. Moreover, even though the suggested rewrite was not a good solution, the information was sufficient to enable the user to fix the error on his or her own.

Out of 1,349 sentences with neutral suggestions that were not accepted, we identified (using a fuzzy match) 215 cases where the user voluntarily modified the sentence so that it contained no flag, without accepting the suggestion. In 44% of these cases, the user had simply typed in the suggested correction instead of accepting it – indicating that true acceptance rates might be higher than we originally estimated. Sixteen percent of the time, the sentence was revised but there remained an error that the system failed to detect. In the other 40% of cases, the voluntary revision improved the sentence. It appears that merely pointing out the possible location of an error to the user is often sufficient to be helpful.

5 Conclusion

In conclusion, judging from the number of people who have visited the *ESL Assistant* web site, there is considerable interest in ESL proofreading tools and services.

When using the tool to proofread text, users do not accept the proposed corrections blindly – they are selective in their behavior. More importantly, they are making informed choices – they can distinguish correct suggestions from incorrect ones. Sometimes identifying the location of an error, even when the solution offered is wrong, itself appears sufficient to cause the user to repair a problem on his or her own. Finally, the user interactions that we have recorded indicate that current state-of-the-art grammatical error correction technology has reached a point where it can be helpful to English language learners in real-world contexts.

Acknowledgments

We thank Bill Dolan, Lucy Vanderwende, Jianfeng Gao, Alexandre Klementiev and Dmitriy Belenko for their contributions to the *ESL Assistant* system. We are also grateful to the two reviewers of this paper who provided valuable feedback.

References

Francis Bond, Kentaro Ogura, and Satoru Ikehara. 1994. Countability and number in Japanese to English machine translation. In *Proceedings of the 15th Conference on Computational Linguistics* (pp. 32-38). Kyoto, Japan.

Martin Chodorow, Michael Gamon, and Joel Tetreault. Under review. The utility of grammatical error detection systems for English language learners: Feedback and Assessment.

Martin Chodorow, Joel Tetreault, and Na-Rae Han. 2007. Detection of grammatical errors involving prepositions. In *Proceedings of the Fourth ACL-SIGSEM Workshop on Prepositions* (pp. 25-30). Prague, Czech Republic.

Rachele De Felice and Stephen G. Pulman. 2007. Automatically acquiring models of preposition use. In *Proceedings of the Fourth ACL-SIGSEM Workshop on Prepositions* (pp. 45-50). Prague, Czech Republic.

Jens Eeg-Olofsson and Ola Knutsson. 2003. Automatic grammar checking for second language learners – the use of prepositions. *Proceedings of NoDaLiDa* 2003. Reykjavik, Iceland.

Michael Gamon, Jianfeng Gao, Chris Brockett, Alexandre Klementiev, William B. Dolan, Dmitriy Belenko, and Lucy Vanderwende. 2008. Using contextual speller techniques and language modeling for ESL error correction. In *Proceedings of the Third International Joint Conference on Natural Language Processing* (pp. 449-455). Hyderabad, India.

Michael Gamon, Claudia Leacock, Chris Brockett, William B. Dolan, Jianfeng Gao, Dmitriy Belenko, and Alexandre Klementiev. 2009. Using statistical techniques and web search to correct ESL errors. To appear in *CALICO Journal, Special Issue on Automatic Analysis of Learner Language*.

Shicun Gui and Huizhong Yan. 2001. Computer analysis of Chinese learner English. Presentation at Hong Kong University of Science and Technology.http://lc.ust.hk/~centre/conf2001/keynote/subsect4/yang.pdf.

Shicun Gui and Huizhong Yang. (Eds.). 2003. *Zhongguo Xuexizhe Yingyu Yuliaohu. (Chinese Learner English Corpus)*. Shanghai Waiyu Jiaoyu Chubanshe. (In Chinese).

Na-Rae Han, Martin Chodorow, and Claudia Leacock 2004). Detecting errors in English article usage with a maximum entropy classifier trained on a large, diverse corpus. In *Proceedings of the 4th International Conference on Language Resources and Evaluation*. Lisbon, Portugal.

Na-Rae Han, Martin Chodorow, and Claudia Leacock 2006. Detecting errors in English article usage by non-native speakers. *Natural Language Engineering*, 12(2), 115-129.

Julia E. Heine. 1998. Definiteness predictions for Japanese noun phrases. In *Proceedings of the 36th Annual Meeting of the Association for Computational Linguistics and 17th International Conference on Computational Linguistics* (pp. 519-525). Montreal, Canada.

Emi Izumi, Kiyotaka Uchimoto, Toyomi Saiga, Thepchai Supnithi, and Hitoshi Isahara. 2003. Automatic error detection in the Japanese learners' English spoken data. In *Proceedings of the 41st Annual Meeting of the Association for Computational Linguistics* (pp. 145-148). Sapporo, Japan.

Kevin Knight and Ishwar Chander,. 1994. Automatic postediting of documents. In *Proceedings of the 12th National Conference on Artificial Intelligence* (pp. 779-784). Seattle: WA.

John Lee. 2004. Automatic article restoration. In *Proceedings of the Human Language Technology Conference of the North American Chapter of the Association for Computational Linguistics* (pp. 31-36). Boston, MA.

John Lee and Stephanie Seneff. 2008. Correcting misuse of verb forms. In *Proceedings of ACl-08/HLT* (pp. 174-182). Columbus, OH.

Guido Minnen, Francis Bond, and Anne Copestake. 2000. Memory-based learning for article generation. In *Proceedings of the Fourth Conference on Computational Natural Language Learning and of the Second Learning Language in Logic Workshop* (pp. 43-48). Lisbon, Portugal.

Masaki Murata and Makoto Nagao. 1993. Determination of referential property and number of nouns in Japanese sentences for machine translation into English. In *Proceedings of the Fifth International Conference on Theoretical and Methodological Issues in Machine Translation* (pp. 218-225). Kyoto, Japan.

Ryo Nagata, Takahiro Wakana, Fumito Masui, Atsui Kawai, and Naoki Isu. 2005. Detecting article errors based on the mass count distinction. In R. Dale, W. Kam-Fie, J. Su and O.Y. Kwong (Eds.) *Natural Language Processing - IJCNLP 2005, Second International Joint Conference Proceedings* (pp. 815-826). New York: Springer.

Ryo Nagata, Atsuo Kawai, Koichiro Morihiro, and Naoki Isu. 2006. A feedback-augmented method for detecting errors in the writing of learners of English. In *Proceedings of the 21st International Conference on Computational Linguistics and 44th Annual Meeting of the Association for Computational Linguistics* (pp. 241-248). Sydney, Australia.

Joel Tetreault and Martin Chodorow. 2008a. The ups and downs of preposition error detection in ESL. COLING. Manchester, UK.

Joel Tetreault and Martin Chodorow. 2008b. Native judgments of non-native usage: Experiments in preposition error detection. In *Proceedings of the Workshop on Human Judgments in Computational Linguistics, 22nd International Conference on Computational Linguistics* (pp 43-48). Manchester, UK.

Jenine Turner and Eugene Charniak. 2007. Language modeling for determiner selection. In *Human Language Technologies 2007: The Conference of the North American Chapter of the Association for Computational Linguistics; Companion Volume, Short Papers* (pp. 177-180). Rochester, NY.

GenERRate: Generating Errors for Use in Grammatical Error Detection

Jennifer Foster
National Centre for Language Technology
School of Computing
Dublin City University, Ireland
jfoster@computing.dcu.ie

Øistein E. Andersen
Computer Laboratory
University of Cambridge
United Kingdom
oa223@cam.ac.uk

Abstract

This paper explores the issue of automatically generated ungrammatical data and its use in error detection, with a focus on the task of classifying a sentence as grammatical or ungrammatical. We present an error generation tool called GenERRate and show how GenERRate can be used to improve the performance of a classifier on learner data. We describe initial attempts to replicate Cambridge Learner Corpus errors using GenERRate.

1 Introduction

In recent years automatically generated ungrammatical data has been used in the training and evaluation of error detection systems, in evaluating the robustness of NLP tools and as negative evidence in unsupervised learning. The main advantage of using such artificial data is that it is cheap to produce. However, it is of little use if it is not a realistic model of the naturally occurring and expensive data that it is designed to replace. In this paper we explore the issues involved in generating synthetic data and present a tool called GenERRate which can be used to produce many different kinds of syntactically noisy data. We use the tool in two experiments in which we attempt to train classifiers to distinguish between grammatical and ungrammatical sentences. In the first experiment, we show how GenERRate can be used to improve the performance of an existing classifier on sentences from a learner corpus of transcribed spoken utterances. In the second experiment we try to produce a synthetic error corpus that is inspired by the Cambridge Learner Corpus (CLC)[1], and we evaluate the difference between a classifier's performance when trained on this data and its performance when trained on original CLC material. The results of both experiments provide pointers on how to improve GenERRate, as well as highlighting some of the challenges associated with automatically generating negative evidence.

The paper is organised as follows: In Section 2, we discuss the reasons why artificial ungrammatical data has been used in NLP and we survey its use in the field, focussing mainly on grammatical error detection. Section 3 contains a description of the GenERRate tool. The two classification experiments which use GenERRate are described in Section 4. Problematic issues are discussed in Section 5 and avenues for future work in Section 6.

2 Background

2.1 Why artifical error data is useful

Before pointing out the benefit of using *artificial* negative evidence in grammatical error detection, it is worth reminding ourselves of the benefits of employing negative evidence, be it artificial or naturally occurring. By grammatical error detection, we mean either the task of distinguishing the grammatical from the ungrammatical at the sentence level or more local targeted error detection, involving the identification, and possibly also correction, of particular types of errors. Distinguishing grammatical utterances from ungrammatical ones involves the use of a binary classifier or a grammaticality scor-

[1] http://www.cambridge.org/elt/corpus/learner_corpus2.htm

Proceedings of the NAACL HLT Workshop on Innovative Use of NLP for Building Educational Applications, pages 82–90,
Boulder, Colorado, June 2009.

ing model. Examples are Andersen (2006; 2007), Okanohara and Tsujii (2007), Sun et al. (2007) and Wagner et al. (2007). In targeted error detection, the focus is on identifying the common errors made either by language learners or native speakers (depending on the application). For ESL applications, this includes the detection of errors involving articles (Han et al., 2006; De Felice and Pulman, 2008; Gamon et al., 2008), prepositions (De Felice and Pulman, 2008; Gamon et al., 2008; Tetreault and Chodorow, 2008), verb forms (Lee and Seneff, 2008b), mass/count noun confusions (Brockett et al., 2006) and word order (Metcalf and Meurers, 2006).

The presence of a pattern in a corpus of well-formed language is positive evidence that the pattern is well-formed. The presence of a pattern in an corpus of ill-formed language is negative evidence that the pattern is erroneous. Discriminative techniques usually lead to more accurate systems than those based on one class alone. The use of the two types of evidence can be seen at work in the system described by Lee and Seneff (2008b): Verb phrases are parsed and their parse trees are examined. If the parse trees resemble the "disturbed" trees that statistical parsers typically produce when an incorrect verb form is used, the verb phrase is considered a likely candidate for correction. However, to avoid overcorrection, positive evidence in the form of Google n-gram statistics is also employed: a correction is only applied if its n-gram frequency is higher than that of the original uncorrected n-gram.

The ideal situation for a grammatical error detection system is one where a large amount of labelled positive *and* negative evidence is available. Depending on the aims of the system, this labelling can range from simply marking a sentence as ungrammatical to a detailed description of the error along with a correction. If an error detection system employs machine learning, the performance of the system will improve as the training set size increases (up to a certain point). For systems which employ learning algorithms with large feature sets (e.g. maximum entropy, support vector machines), the size of the training set is particularly important so that overfitting is avoided. The collection of a large corpus of ungrammatical data requires a good deal of manual effort. Even if the annotation only involves marking the sentence as correct/incorrect, it still requires that the sentence be read and a grammaticality judgement applied to it. If more detailed annotation is applied, the process takes even longer. Some substantially-sized annotated error corpora do exist, e.g. the Cambridge Learner Corpus, but these are not freely available.

One way around this problem of lack of availability of suitably large error-annotated corpora is to introduce errors into sentences automatically. In order for the resulting error corpus to be useful in an error detection system, the errors that are introduced need to resemble those that the system aims to detect. Thus, the process is not without some manual effort: knowing what kind of errors to introduce requires the inspection of real error data, a process similar to error annotation. Once the error types have been specified though, the process is fully automatic and allows large error corpora to be compiled. If the set of well-formed sentences into which the errors are introduced is large and varied enough, it is possible that this will result in ungrammatical sentence structures which learners produce but which have not yet been recorded in the smaller naturally occurring learner corpora. To put it another way, the same type of error will appear in lexically and syntactically varied *contexts*, which is potentially advantageous when training a classifier.

2.2 Where artificial error data has been used

Artificial errors have been employed previously in targeted error detection. Sjöbergh and Knutsson (2005) introduce split compound errors and word order errors into Swedish texts and use the resulting artificial data to train their error detection system. These two particular error types are chosen because they are frequent errors amongst non-native Swedish speakers whose first language does not contain compounds or has a fixed word order. They compare the resulting system to three Swedish grammar checkers, and find that their system has higher recall at the expense of lower precision. Brockett et al. (2006) introduce errors involving mass/count noun confusions into English newswire text and then use the resulting parallel corpus to train a phrasal SMT system to perform error correction. Lee and Seneff (2008b) automatically introduce verb form errors (subject–verb agreement errors, complementation errors and errors in a main verb after an auxiliary) into well-formed text, parse the resulting text and examine the parse trees produced.

Both Okanohara and Tsujii (2007) and Wagner et al. (2007) attempt to learn a model which discriminates between grammatical and ungrammatical sentences, and both use synthetic negative data which is obtained by distorting sentences from the British National Corpus (BNC) (Burnard, 2000). The methods used to distort the BNC sentences are, however, quite different. Okanohara and Tsujii (2007) generate ill-formed sentences by sampling a probabilistic language model and end up with "pseudo-negative" examples which resemble machine translation output more than they do learner texts. Indeed, machine translation is one of the applications of their resulting discriminative language model. Wagner et al. (2007) introduce grammatical errors of the following four types into BNC sentences: context-sensitive spelling errors, agreement errors, errors involving a missing word and errors involving an extra word. All four types are considered equally likely and the resulting synthetic corpus contains errors that look like the kind of slips that would be made by native speakers (e.g. repeated adjacent words) as well as errors that resemble learner errors (e.g. missing articles). Wagner et al. (2009) report a drop in accuracy for their classification methods when applied to real learner texts as opposed to held-out synthetic test data, reinforcing the earlier point that artificial errors need to be tailored for the task at hand (we return to this in Section 4.1).

Artificial error data has also proven useful in the automatic evaluation of error detection systems. Bigert (2004) describes how a tool called Missplel is used to generate context-sensitive spelling errors which are then used to evaluate a context-sensitive spelling error detection system. The performance of general-purpose NLP tools such as part-of-speech taggers and parsers in the face of noisy ungrammatical data has been automatically evaluated using artificial error data. Since the features of machine-learned error detectors are often part-of-speech n-grams or word–word dependencies extracted from parser output (De Felice and Pulman, 2008, for example), it is important to understand how part-of-speech taggers and parsers react to particular grammatical errors. Bigert et al. (2005) introduce artificial context-sensitive spelling errors into error-free Swedish text and then evaluate parsers and a part-of-speech tagger on this text using their performance on the error-free text as a reference. Similarly, Foster (2007) investigates the effect of common English grammatical errors on two widely-used statistical parsers using distorted treebank trees as references. The procedure used by Wagner et al. (2007; 2009) is used to introduce errors into the treebank sentences.

Finally, negative evidence in the form of automatically distorted sentences has been used in unsupervised learning. Smith and Eisner (2005a; 2005b) generate negative evidence for their *contrastive estimation* method by moving or removing a word in a sentence. Since the aim of this work is not to detect grammatical errors, there is no requirement to generate the kind of negative evidence that might actually be produced by either native or non-native speakers of a language. The negative examples are used to guide the unsupervised learning of a part-of-speech tagger and a dependency grammar.

We can conclude from this survey that synthetic error data *is* useful in a variety of NLP applications, including error detection and evaluation of error detectors. In Section 3, we describe an automatic error generation tool, which has a modular design and is flexible enough to accommodate the generation of the various types of synthetic data described above.

3 Error Generation Tool

GenERRate is an error generation tool which accepts as input a corpus and an *error analysis* file consisting of a list of errors and produces an error-tagged corpus of syntactically ill-formed sentences. The sentences in the input corpus are assumed to be grammatically well-formed. GenERRate is implemented in Java and will be made available to download for use by other researchers.[2]

3.1 Supported Error Types

Error types are defined in terms of their corrections, that is, in terms of the operations (*insert, delete, substitute* and *move*) that are applied to a well-formed sentence to make it ill-formed. As well as being a popular classification scheme in the field of error analysis (James, 1998), it has the advantage of

[2] `http://www.computing.dcu.ie/~jfoster/resources/generrate.html`

being theory-neutral. This is important in this context since it is hoped that GenERRate will be used to create negative evidence of various types, be it L2-like grammatical errors, native speaker slips or more random syntactic noise. It is hoped that GenERRate will be easy to use for anyone working in linguistics, applied linguistics, language teaching or computational linguistics.

The inheritance hierarchy in Fig. 1 shows the error types that are supported by GenERRate. We briefly describe each error type.

Errors generated by removing a word

- **DeletionError:** Generated by selecting a word at random from the sentence and removing it.
- **DeletionPOSError:** Extends DeletionError by allowing a specific POS to be specified.
- **DeletionPOSWhereError:** Extends DeletionPOSError by allowing left and/or right context (POS tag or *start/end*) to be specified.

Errors generated by inserting a word

- **InsertionError:** Insert a random word at a random position. The word is chosen either from the sentence itself or from a word list, and this choice is also random.
- **InsertionFromFileOrSentenceError:** This differs from the InsertionError in that the decision of whether to use the sentence itself or a word list is not made at random but supplied in the error type specification.
- **InsertionPOSError:** Extends InsertionFromFileOrSentenceError by allowing the POS of the new word to be specified.
- **InsertionPOSWhereError:** Analogous to the DeletionPOSWhereError, this extends InsertionPOSError by allowing left and/or right context to be specified.

Errors generated by moving a word

- **MoveError:** Generated by randomly selecting a word in the sentence and moving it to another position, randomly chosen, in the sentence.
- **MovePOSError:** A word tagged with the specified POS is randomly chosen and moved to a randomly chosen position in the sentence.
- **MovePOSWhereError:** Extends MovePOSError by allowing the change in position to be specified in terms of direction and number of words.

```
subst,word,an,a,0.2
subst,NNS,NN,0.4
subst,VBG,TO,0.2
delete,DT,0.1
move,RB,left,1,0.1
```

Figure 2: GenERRate Toy Error Analysis File

Errors generated by substituting a word

- **SubstError:** Replace a random word by a word chosen at random from a word list.
- **SubstWordConfusionError:** Extends SubstError by allowing the POS to be specified (same POS for both words).
- **SubstWordConfusionNewPOSError:** Similar to SubstWordConfusionError, but allows different POSs to be specified.
- **SubstSpecificWordConfusionError:** Replace a specific word with another (e.g. *be/have*).
- **SubstWrongFormError:** Replace a word with a different form of the same word. The following changes are currently supported: noun number (e.g. *word/words*), verb number (*write/writes*), verb form (*writing/written*), adjective form (*big/bigger*) and adjective/adverb (*quick/quickly*). Note that this is the only error type which is language-specific. At the moment, only English is supported.

3.2 Input Corpus

The corpus that is supplied as input to GenERRate must be split into sentences. It does not have to be part-of-speech tagged, but it will not be possible to generate many of the errors if it is not. GenERRate has been tested using two part-of-speech tagsets, the Penn Treebank tagset (Santorini, 1991) and the CLAWS tagset (Garside et al., 1987).

3.3 Error Analysis File

The error analysis file specifies the errors that GenERRate should attempt to insert into the sentences in the input corpus. A toy example with the Penn tagset is shown in Fig. 2. The first line is an instance of a *SubstSpecificWordConfusion* error. The second

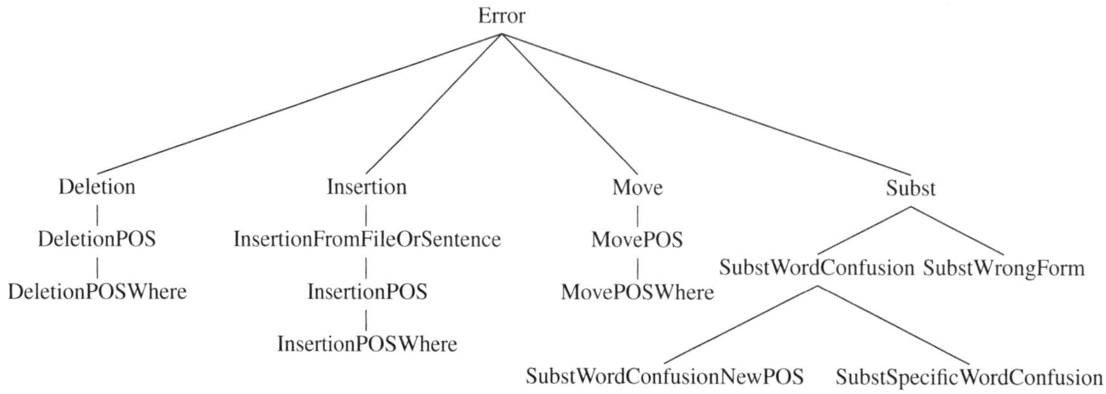

Figure 1: GenERRate Error Types

and third are instances of the *SubstWrongFormError* type. The fourth is a *DeletionPOSError*, and the fifth is a *MovePOSWhereError*. The number in the final column specifies the desired proportion of the particular error type in the output corpus and is optional. However, if it is present for one error type, it must be present for all. The overall size of the output corpus is supplied as a parameter when running GenERRate.

3.4 Error Generation

When frequency information is not supplied in the error analysis file, GenERRate iterates through each error in the error analysis file and each sentence in the input corpus, tries to insert an error of this type into the sentence and writes the resulting sentence to the output file together with a description of the error. GenERRate includes an option to write the sentences into which an error could not be inserted and the reason for the failure to a log file. When the error analysis file *does* include frequency information, a slightly different algorithm is used: for each error, GenERRate selects sentences from the input file and attempts to generate an instance of that error until the desired number of errors has been produced or all sentences have been tried.

4 Classification Experiments

We describe two experiments which involve the use of GenERRate in a binary classification task in which the classifiers attempt to distinguish between grammatically well-formed and ill-formed sentences or, more precisely, to distinguish between sentences in learner corpora which have been annotated as erroneous and their corrected counterparts. In the first experiment we use GenERRate to create ungrammatical training data using information about error types gleaned from a subset of a corpus of transcribed spoken utterances produced by ESL learners in a classroom environment. The classifier is one of those described in Wagner et al. (2007). In the second experiment we try to generate a CLC-inspired error corpus and we use one of the simplest classifiers described in Andersen (2006). Our aim is not to improve classification performance, but to test the GenERRate tool, to demonstrate how it can be used and to investigate differences between synthetic and naturally occurring datasets.

4.1 Experiments with a Spoken Language Learner Corpus

Wagner et al. (2009) train various classifiers to distinguish between BNC sentences and artificially produced ungrammatical versions of BNC sentences (see §2). They report a significant drop in accuracy when they apply these classifiers to real learner data, including the sentences in a corpus of transcribed spoken utterances. The aim of this experiment is to investigate to what extent this loss in accuracy can be reduced by using GenERRate to produce a more realistic set of ungrammatical training examples.

The spoken language learner corpus contains over 4,000 transcribed spoken sentences which were produced by learners of English of all levels and with a variety of L1s. The sentences were produced in a classroom setting and transcribed by the teacher. The transcriptions were verified by the students. All of the utterances have been marked as erroneous.

4.1.1 Setup

A 200-sentence held-out section of the corpus is analysed by hand and a GenERRate error analysis file containing 89 errors is compiled. The most frequent errors are those involving a change in noun or verb number or an article deletion. GenERRate then applies this error analysis file to 440,930 BNC sentences resulting in the same size set of synthetic examples ("new-ungram-BNC"). Another set of synthetic sentences ("old-ungram-BNC") is produced from the same input using the error generation procedure used by Wagner et al. (2007; 2009). Table 1 shows examples from both sets.

Two classifiers are then trained, one on the original BNC sentences and the old-ungram-BNC sentences, and the other on the original BNC sentences and the new-ungram-BNC sentences. Both classifiers are tested on 4,095 sentences from the spoken language corpus (excluding the held-out section). 310 of these sentences are corrected, resulting in a small set of grammatical test data. The classifier used is the POS n-gram frequency classifier described in Wagner et al. (2007).[3] The features are the frequencies of the least frequent n-grams (2–7) in the input sentence. The BNC (excluding those sentences that are used as training data) is used as reference data to compute the frequencies. Learning is carried out using the *Weka* implementation of the J48 decision tree algorithm.[4]

4.1.2 Results

The results of the experiment are displayed in Table 2. The evaluation measures used are precision, recall, total accuracy and accuracy on the grammatical side of the test data. Recall is the same as accuracy on the ungrammatical side of the test data.

The results are encouraging. There is a significant increase in accuracy when we train on the new-ungram-BNC set instead of the old-ungram-BNC set. This increase is on the ungrammatical side of the test data, i.e. an increase in recall, demonstrating that by analysing a small set of data from our test domain, we can automatically create more effective training data. This is useful in a scenario where a small-to-medium-sized learner corpus is available but which is not large enough to be split into a training/development/test set. These results seem to indicate that reasonably useful training data can be created with minimum effort. Of course, the accuracy is still rather low but we suspect that some of this difference can be explained by domain effects — the sentences in the training data are BNC written sentences (or distorted versions of them) whereas the sentences in the learner corpus are transcribed spoken utterances. Re-running the experiments using the spoken language section of the BNC as training data might yield better results.

4.2 A CLC-Inspired Corpus

We investigate to what extent it is possible to create a large error corpus inspired by the CLC using the current version of GenERRate. The CLC is a 30-million-word corpus of learner English collected from University of Cambridge ESOL exam papers at different levels. Approximately 50% of the CLC has been annotated for errors and corrected.

4.2.1 Setup

We attempt to use GenERRate to insert errors into corrected CLC sentences. In order to do this, we need to create a CLC-specific error analysis file. In contrast to the previous experiment, we do this *automatically* by extracting erroneous POS trigrams from the error-annotated CLC sentences and encoding them as GenERRate errors. This results in approximately 13,000 errors of the following types: DeletionPOSWhereError, InsertionPOSWhereError, MovePOSWhereError, SubstWordConfusionError, SubstWordConfusionNewPOSError, SubstSpecificWordConfusionError and SubstWrongFormError. Frequencies are extracted, and errors occurring only once are excluded.

Three classifiers are trained. The first is trained on corrected CLC sentences (the grammatical section of the training set) and original CLC sentences (the ungrammatical section). The second classifier is trained on corrected CLC sentences and the sentences that are generated from the corrected CLC

[3] Wagner et al. (2009) report accuracy figures in the range 55–70% for their various classifiers (when tested on synthetic test data), but the best performance is obtained by combining parser-output and n-gram POS frequency features using decision trees in a voting scheme.

[4] http://www.cs.waikato.ac.nz/ml/weka/

Old-Ungram-BNC	New-Ungram-BNC
Biogas ***production production*** *is growing rapidly*	*Biogas* ***productions*** *is growing rapidly*
Emil ***as*** *courteous and helpful*	*Emil courteous and* ***was*** *helpful*
I ***knows*** *what makes you tick*	*I know what* ***make*** *you tick*
He did n't bother to lift his eyes from the ***task hand***	*He did n't bother* ***lift*** *his eyes from the task at hand*

Table 1: Examples from two synthetic BNC sets

Training Data	Precision	Recall	Accuracy	Accuracy on Grammatical
BNC/old-ungram-BNC	95.5	37.0	39.8	76.8
BNC/new-ungram-BNC	94.9	51.6	52.4	63.2

Table 2: Spoken Language Learner Corpus Classification Experiment

sentences using GenERRate (we call these "faux-CLC"). The third is trained on corrected CLC sentences and a 50/50 combination of CLC and faux-CLC sentences. In all experiments, the grammatical section of the training data contains 438,150 sentences and the ungrammatical section 454,337. The classifiers are tested on a held-out section of the CLC containing 43,639 corrected CLC sentences and 45,373 original CLC sentences. To train the classifiers, the *Mallet* implementation of Naive Bayes is used.[5] The features are word unigrams and bigrams, as well as part-of-speech unigrams, bigrams and trigrams. Andersen (2006) experimented with various learning algorithms and, taking into account training time and performance, found Naive Bayes to be optimal. The POS-tagging is carried out by the RASP system (Briscoe and Carroll, 2002).

4.2.2 Results

The results of the CLC classification experiment are presented in Table 3. There is a 6.2% drop in accuracy when we move from training on original CLC sentences to artificially generated sentences. This is somewhat disappointing since it means that we have not completely succeeded in replicating the CLC errors using GenERRate. Most of the accuracy drop is on the ungrammatical side, i.e. the correct/faux model classifies more incorrect CLC sentences as correct than the correct/incorrect model. This drop in accuracy occurs because some frequently occurring error types are not included in the error analysis file. One reason for the gap in coverage is the failure of the part-of-speech tagset to make some important distinctions. The corrected CLC sentences which were used to generate the faux-CLC set were tagged with the CLAWS tagset, and although more fine-grained than the Penn tagset, it does not, for example, make a distinction between mass and count nouns, a common source of error. Another important reason for the drop in accuracy are the recurrent spelling errors which occur in the incorrect CLC test set but not in the faux-CLC test set. It is promising, however, that much of the performance degradation is recovered when a mixture of the two types of ungrammatical training data is used, suggesting that artificial data could be used to augment naturally occurring training sets

5 Limitations of GenERRate

We present three issues that make the task of generating synthetic error data non-trivial.

5.1 Sophistication of Input Format

The experiments in §4 highlight coverage issues with GenERRate, some of which are due to the simplicity of the supported error types. When linguistic context is supplied for deletion or insertion errors, it takes the form of the POS of the words immediately to the left and/or right of the target word. Lee and Seneff (2008a) analysed preposition errors made by Japanese learners of English and found that a greater proportion of errors in argument prepositional phrases (*look at him*) involved a deletion than those in adjunct PPs (*came at night*). The only way for such a distinction to be encoded in a GenERRate error analysis file is to allow *parsed* input to be accepted. This brings with it the problem, however, that parsers are less accurate than POS-taggers. Another possible improvement would be to make use

[5] http://mallet.cs.umass.edu/

Training Data	Precision	Recall	Accuracy	Accuracy on Grammatical
Held-Out Test Data				
Correct/Incorrect CLC	69.7	42.6	61.3	80.8
Correct/Faux CLC	62.0	30.7	55.1	80.5
Correct/Incorrect+Faux CLC	69.7	38.2	60.0	82.7

Table 3: CLC Classification Experiment

of WordNet synsets in order to choose the new word in substitution errors.

5.2 Covert Errors

A covert error is an error that results in a syntactically well-formed sentence with an interpretation different from the intended one. Covert errors are a natural phenomenon, occurring in real corpora. Lee and Seneff (2008b) give the example *I am preparing for the exam* which has been annotated as erroneous because, given its context, it is clear that the person meant to write *I am prepared for the exam*. The problems lie in deciding what covert errors should be handled by an error detection system and how to create synthetic data which gets the balance right.

When to avoid: Covert errors can be produced by GenERRate as a result of the sparse linguistic context provided for an error in the error analysis file. An inspection of the new-ungram-BNC set shows that some error types are more likely to result in covert errors. An example is the *SubstWrongFormError* when it is used to change a noun from singular to plural. This results in the sentence *But there was no sign of Benny's father* being changed to the well-formed but more implausible *But there was no sign of Benny's* ***fathers***. The next version of GenERRate should include the option to change the form of a word *in a certain context*.

When not to avoid: In the design of GenERRate, particularly in the design of the *SubstWrongFormError* type, the decision was made to exclude tense errors because they are likely to result in covert errors, e.g. *She walked home* → *She* ***walks*** *home*. But in doing so we also avoid generating examples like this one from the spoken language learner corpus: *When I was a high school student, I* ***go*** *to bed at one o'clock*. These tense errors are common in L2 data and their omission from the faux-CLC training set is one of the reasons why the performance of this model is inferior to the real-CLC model.

5.3 More complex errors

The learner corpora contain some errors that are corrected by applying more than one transformation. Some are handled by the *SubstWrongFormError* type (*I spend a long time* ***to fish*** →*I spend a long time* ***fishing***) but some are not (*She is one of* ***reason*** *I became interested in English* → *She is one of* ***the reasons*** *I became interested in English*).

6 Conclusion

We have presented GenERRate, a tool for automatically introducing syntactic errors into sentences and shown how it can be useful for creating synthetic training data to be used in grammatical error detection research. Although we have focussed on the binary classification task, we also intend to test GenERRate in targeted error detection. Another avenue for future work is to explore whether GenERRate could be of use in the automatic generation of language test items (Chen et al., 2006, for example). Our immediate aim is to produce a new version of GenERRate which tackles some of the coverage issues highlighted by our experiments.

Acknowledgments

This paper reports on research supported by the University of Cambridge ESOL Examinations. We are very grateful to Cambridge University Press for giving us access to the Cambridge Learner Corpus and to James Hunter from Gonzaga College for supplying us with the spoken language learner corpus. We thank Ted Briscoe, Josef van Genabith, Joachim Wagner and the reviewers for their very helpful suggestions.

References

Øistein E. Andersen. 2006. Grammatical error detection. Master's thesis, Cambridge University.

Øistein E. Andersen. 2007. Grammatical error detection using corpora and supervised learning. In Ville Nurmi and Dmitry Sustretov, editors, *Proceedings of the 12th Student Session of the European Summer School for Logic, Language and Information*, Dublin.

Johnny Bigert, Jonas Sjöbergh, Ola Knutsson, and Magnus Sahlgren. 2005. Unsupervised evaluation of parser robustness. In *Proceedings of the 6th CICling*, Mexico City.

Johnny Bigert. 2004. Probabilistic detection of context-sensitive spelling errors. In *Proceedings of the 4th LREC*, Lisbon.

Ted Briscoe and John Carroll. 2002. Robust accurate statistical annotation of general text. In *Proceedings of the 3rd LREC*, Las Palmas.

Chris Brockett, William B. Dolan, and Michael Gamon. 2006. Correcting ESL errors using phrasal SMT techniques. In *Proceedings of the 21st COLING and the 44th ACL*, Sydney.

Lou Burnard. 2000. User reference guide for the British National Corpus. Technical report, Oxford University Computing Services.

Chia-Yin Chen, Liou Hsien-Chin, and Jason S. Chang. 2006. Fast — an automatic generation system for grammar tests. In *Proceedings of the COLING/ACL 2006 Interactive Presentation Sessions*, Sydney.

Rachele De Felice and Stephen G. Pulman. 2008. A classifier-based approach to preposition and determiner error correction in L2 English. In *Proceedings of the 22nd COLING*, Manchester.

Jennifer Foster. 2007. Treebanks gone bad: Parser evaluation and retraining using a treebank of ungrammatical sentences. *International Journal on Document Analysis and Recognition*, 10(3-4):129–145.

Michael Gamon, Jianfeng Gao, Chris Brockett, Alexandre Klementiev, William B. Dolan, Dmitriy Belenko, and Lucy Vanderwende. 2008. Using contextual speller techniques and language modelling for ESL error correction. In *Proceedings of the 3rd IJCNLP*, Hyderabad.

Roger Garside, Geoffrey Leech, and Geoffrey Sampson, editors. 1987. *The Computational Analysis of English: a Corpus-Based Approach*. Longman, London.

Na-Rae Han, Martin Chodorow, and Claudia Leacock. 2006. Detecting errors in English article usage by non-native speakers. *Natural Language Engineering*, 12(2):115–129.

Carl James. 1998. *Errors in Language Learning and Use: Exploring Error Analysis*. Addison Wesley Longman.

John Lee and Stephanie Seneff. 2008a. An analysis of grammatical errors in non-native speech in English. In *Proceedings of the 2008 Spoken Language Technology Workshop*, Goa.

John Lee and Stephanie Seneff. 2008b. Correcting misuse of verb forms. In *Proceedings of the 46th ACL*, Columbus.

Vanessa Metcalf and Detmar Meurers. 2006. Towards a treatment of word order errors: When to use deep processing – and when not to. Presentation at the NLP in CALL Workshop, CALICO 2006.

Daisuke Okanohara and Jun'ichi Tsujii. 2007. A discriminative language model with pseudo-negative samples. In *Proceedings of the 45th ACL*, Prague.

Beatrice Santorini. 1991. Part-of-speech tagging guidelines for the Penn Treebank project. Technical report, University of Pennsylvania, Philadelphia, PA.

Jonas Sjöbergh and Ola Knutsson. 2005. Faking errors to avoid making errors. In *Proceedings of RANLP 2005*, Borovets.

Noah A. Smith and Jason Eisner. 2005a. Contrastive Estimation: Training log-linear models on unlabeled data. In *Proceedings of the 43rd ACL*, Ann Arbor.

Noah A. Smith and Jason Eisner. 2005b. Guiding unsupervised grammar induction using contrastive estimation. In *Proceedings of the IJCAI Workshop on Grammatical Inference Applications*, Edinburgh.

Guihua Sun, Xiaohua Liu, Gao Cong, Ming Zhou, Zhongyang Xiong, John Lee, and Chin-Yew Lin. 2007. Detecting erroneous sentences using automatically mined sequential patterns. In *Proceedings of the 45rd ACL*, Prague.

Joel R. Tetreault and Martin Chodorow. 2008. The ups and downs of preposition error detection in ESL writing. In *Proceedings of the 22nd COLING*, Manchester.

Joachim Wagner, Jennifer Foster, and Josef van Genabith. 2007. A comparative evaluation of deep and shallow approaches to the automatic detection of common grammatical errors. In *Proceedings of the joint EMNLP/CoNLL*, Prague.

Joachim Wagner, Jennifer Foster, and Josef van Genabith. 2009. Judging grammaticality: Experiments in sentence classification. *CALICO Journal*. Special Issue on the 2008 Automatic Analysis of Learner Language CALICO Workshop. To Appear.